Spanish

Complete Revision and Practice

Niobe O'Connor

Published by BBC Active, an imprint of Educational Publishers LLP, part of the Pearson Education Group Edinburgh Gate, Harlow, Essex CN20 2JE, England

Text copyright © Niobe O'Connor/BBC Worldwide Ltd, 2002

Design & concept copyright © BBC Worldwide Ltd, 2002, 2004/BBC Active 2010

BBC logo © BBC 1996. BBC and BBC Active are trademarks of the British Broadcasting Corporation

ISBN 978-1-4066-5448-6

Printed in China CTPSC/01

The Publisher's policy is to use paper manufactured from sustainable forests.

First published 2002

This edition 2010

Minimum recommended system requirements
PC: Windows(r), XP sp2, Pentium 4 1 GHz processor (2 GHz for Vista), 512 MB of RAM (1 GB for Windows Vista), 1 GB of free hard disk space, CD-ROM drive 16x, 16 bit colour monitor set at 1024 x 768 pixels resolution
MAC: Mac OS X 10.3.9 or higher, G4 processor at 1 GHz or faster, 512 MB RAM, 1 GB free space (or 10% of drive capacity, whichever is higher), Microsoft Internet Explorer® 6.1 SP2 or Macintosh Safari™ 1.3, Adobe Flash® Player 9 or higher, Adobe Reader® 7 or higher, Headphones recommended

If you experiencing difficulty in launching the enclosed CD-ROM, or in accessing content, please review the following notes:
1 Ensure your computer meets the minimum requirements. Faster machines will improve performance.
2 If the CD does not automatically open, Windows users should open 'My Computer', double-click on the CD icon, then the file named 'launcher.exe'. Macintosh users should double-click on the CD icon, then 'launcher.osx'
Please note: the eDesktop Revision Planner is provided as-is and cannot be supported.
For other technical support, visit the following address for articles which may help resolve your issues:
http://centraal.uk.knowledgebox.com/kbase/

If you cannot find information which helps you to resolve your particular issue, please email: Digital.Support@pearson.com.
Please include the following information in your mail:
- Your name and daytime telephone number.
- ISBN of the product (found on the packaging.)
- Details of the problem you are experiencing - e.g. how to reproduce the problem, any error messages e
- Details of your computer (operating system, RAM, processor type and speed if known.)

210 045 771

Contents

Personal and family life

Home and local community

Media, culture and holidays

Study, work and employment

* Only available in the CD-ROM version of the book.

Exam board specification map

Provides a quick and easy overview of the topics you need to study for the examinations you will be taking.

Topics	AQA	CCEA	Edexel	OCR	WJEC
Personal and family life					
Vocabulary	✓	✓	✓	✓	✓
Grammar	✓	✓	✓	✓	✓
Self, family and friends	✓	✓	✓	✓	✓
Daily routine	✓	✓	✓	✓	✓
Relationships	✓	✓	✓	✓	✓
Vocabulary/Grammar	✓	✓	✓	✓	✓
Interests and hobbies	✓	✓	✓	✓	✓
Healthy living	✓	✓	✓	✓	✓
Mealtimes and special occasions	✓	✓	✓	✓	✓
New technology	✓	✓	✓	✓	✓
Listening section A	✓	✓	✓	✓	✓
Home and local community					
Vocabulary	✓	✓	✓	✓	✓
Grammar	✓	✓	✓	✓	✓
My home and bedroom	✓	✓		✓	✓
Local area	✓	✓	✓	✓	✓
Tourist information	✓	✓	✓	✓	✓
Weather and climate	✓	✓	✓	✓	✓
Vocabulary/Grammar	✓	✓	✓	✓	✓
Finding the way	✓	✓	✓	✓	✓
Travel and transport	✓	✓	✓	✓	✓
The environment	✓	✓	✓	✓	✓
Listening section B	✓	✓	✓	✓	✓

Topics	AQA	CCEA	Edexel	OCR	WJEC
Media, culture and holidays					
Vocabulary	✓	✓	✓	✓	✓
Grammar	✓	✓	✓	✓	✓
Going out, TV and films	✓	✓	✓	✓	✓
Popular culture	✓	✓	✓	✓	✓
Shopping	✓	✓	✓	✓	✓
Holiday activities	✓	✓	✓	✓	✓
Vocabulary/Grammar	✓	✓	✓	✓	✓
Accommodation	✓	✓	✓	✓	✓
Services	✓	✓	✓	✓	✓
Staying in touch	✓	✓	✓	✓	✓
Listening section C	✓	✓	✓	✓	✓
Study, work and employment					
Vocabulary	✓	✓	✓	✓	✓
Grammar	✓	✓	✓	✓	✓
School and after the exams	✓	✓	✓	✓	✓
Part-time jobs	✓	✓	✓	✓	✓
Education issues	✓	✓	✓	✓	✓
Vocabulary/Grammar	✓	✓	✓	✓	✓
Work experience	✓	✓	✓	✓	✓
CVs and applying for a job	✓	✓	✓	✓	✓
Future work	✓	✓	✓	✓	✓
Social concerns	✓	✓		✓	✓
Listening section D	✓	✓	✓	✓	✓
Exam questions and model answers	✓	✓	✓	✓	✓
Complete the grammar	✓	✓	✓	✓	✓
Vocabulary extra	✓	✓	✓	✓	✓

Introduction

How to use GCSE Bitesize Complete Revision and Practice

Begin with the CD-ROM. There are five easy steps to using the CD-ROM – and to creating your own personal revision programme. Follow these steps and you'll be fully prepared for the exam without wasting time on areas you already know.

Topic checker

Step 1: Check

The Topic checker will help you figure out what you know – and what you need to revise.

Revision planner

Step 2: Plan

When you know which topics you need to revise, enter them into the handy Revision planner. You'll get a daily reminder to make sure you're on track.

Step 3: Revise

From the Topic checker, you can go straight to the topic pages that contain all the facts you need to know.

- Give yourself the edge with the Web*Bite* buttons. These link directly to the relevant section on the BBC Bitesize Revision website.

- Audio*Bite* buttons let you listen to more about the topic to boost your knowledge even further. *

Step 4: Practise

Check your understanding by answering the Practice questions. Click on each question to see the correct answer.

Step 5: Exam

Are you ready for the exam? Exam*Bite* buttons take you to an exam question on the topics you've just revised. *

* Not all subjects contain these features, depending on their exam requirements.

Interactive book
You can choose to go through every topic from beginning to end by clicking on the Interactive book and selecting topics on the Contents page.

 Exam questions
Find all of the exam questions in one place by clicking on the Exam questions tab.

 Last-minute learner
The Last-minute learner gives you the most important facts in a few pages for that final revision session.

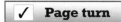
You can access the information on these pages at any time from the link on the Topic checker or by clicking on the Help button. You can also do the Tutorial which provides step-by-step instructions on how to use the CD-ROM and gives you an overview of all the features available. You can find the Tutorial on the Home page when you click on the Home button.

Other features include:

Click on the draw tool to annotate pages. N.B. Annotations cannot be saved.

 Page turn
Click on Page turn to stop the pages turning over like a book.

Click on the Single page icon to see a single page.

Click on this arrow to go back to the previous screen.

Contents
Click on Contents while in the Interactive book to see a contents list in a pop-up window.

◄ ►
Click on these arrows to go backward or forward one page at a time.

Click on this bar to switch the buttons to the opposite side of the screen.

Click on any section of the text on a topic page to zoom in for a closer look.

N.B. You may come across some exercises that you can't do on-screen, such as circling or underlining, in these cases you should use the printed book.

About this book

Use this book whenever you prefer to work away from your computer. It consists of two main parts:

 A set of double-page spreads, covering the essential topics for revision from each of the curriculum areas. Each topic is organised in the following way:

- A summary of the main points and an introduction to the topic.

- Lettered section boxes cover the important areas within each topic.

- Key facts are clearly highlighted – these indicate the essential information in a section or give you tips on answering exam questions.

- Practice questions at the end of each topic – a range of questions to check your understanding.

 A number of special sections to help you consolidate your revision and get a feel for how exam questions are structured and marked. These extra sections will help you check your progress and be confident that you know your stuff.
They include:

- A selection of exam-style questions and worked model answers and comments to help you get full marks.

- Topic checker – quick questions covering all topic areas.

- Complete the grammar – check that you have the most important grammar at your fingertips.

- Last-minute learner – the most important facts in just in a few pages.

About your exam

Get organised

You need to know when your exams are before you make your revision plan. Check the dates, times and locations of your exams with your teacher, tutor or school office.

On the day

Aim to arrive in plenty of time, with everything you need: several pens, pencils, a ruler, and possibly mathematical instruments, a calculator, or a language dictionary, depending on the exam subject.

On your way or while you're waiting, read through your Last-minute learner.

In the exam room

When you are issued with your exam paper, you must not open it immediately. However, there are some details on the front cover that you can fill in (your name, centre number, etc.) before you start the exam itself. If you're not sure where to write these details, ask one of the invigilators (teachers supervising the exam).

When it's time to begin writing, read each question carefully. Remember to keep an eye on the time.

Finally, don't panic! If you have followed your teacher's advice and the suggestions in this book, you will be well-prepared for any question on your exam.

Topic checker

Go through these questions after you've revised a group of topics, putting a tick if you know the answer.

Personal information (pp. 2, 6)

1	Can you say what your name is, and spell it? (p. 2)	☐
2	Can you say the Spanish alphabet? (p. 2)	☐
3	Can you say what age you are and when your birthday is? (p. 2)	☐
4	Can you say what nationality you are? (p. 2)	☐
5	Can you ask someone else for personal information? (p. 2)	☐

Family and friends

6	Can you talk about who is in your family? (p. 2)	☐
7	Can you say that someone is an only son/daughter? (p. 2)	☐
8	Can you describe someone's relationship status (e.g. married, divorced)? (p. 2)	☐
9	Can you talk about your wider family (e.g. uncle, grandmother)? (p. 2)	☐

Character and relationships (pp. 3, 10–11)

10	Can you describe your own character and someone else's? (pp. 3, 10)	☐
11	Can you say what you think a good friend should be like? (p. 3)	☐
12	Can you say how well you get on with different members of your family? (p. 3)	☐
13	Can you describe how someone else behaves? (p. 3)	☐
14	Can you talk about your thoughts on future relationships? (pp. 10–11)	☐

Daily routine and helping at home (pp. 8–9)

15	Can you describe your daily routine during the week? (p. 8)	☐
16	Can you talk about someone else's routine? (p. 8)	☐
17	Can you say what you and others do to help out at home? (p. 9)	☐

Interests and hobbies (pp. 12, 14–15)

18	Can you say what sports you play? (p. 12, 14)	☐
19	Can you explain what other things you do in your free time? (pp. 12, 14)	☐
20	Can you say whether you play a musical instrument or not? (p. 12)	☐
21	Can you talk about what you like, or don't like? (pp. 13–14)	☐
22	Can you ask others about sports or hobbies they do? (p. 12)	☐
23	Can you say how you use the Internet? (p. 12, 15)	☐
24	Can you explain when and how often you do an activity? (p. 15)	☐

Healthy living (pp. 12, 16)

25	Can you explain how to stay healthy? (pp. 12, 16)	☐
26	Can you describe what is good and bad for health? (pp. 12, 16–17)	☐
27	Can you say what you should and should not eat? (pp. 12)	☐
28	Can you talk about the dangers of smoking, drinking and taking drugs? (pp. 12, 17)	☐

Mealtimes and special occasions (pp. 18–19)

29	Can you say which special occasions you celebrate at home? (p. 18)	☐
30	Can you describe what you do to celebrate? (p. 18)	☐
31	Can you talk about mealtimes and which foods you like and dislike? (p. 19)	☐

New technologies (pp. 12, 15, 20–21)

32	Can you say which aspects of new technologies you use? (p. 12, 15, 20)	☐
33	Can you explain the advantages of new technologies? (p. 12, 15, 20–21)	☐
34	Can you give your views on the disadvantages of the Internet? (p. 12, 15, 20–21)	☐

Topic checker

Topic checker

My home and town/village (pp. 24–25, 29–31)

35	Can you say what type of house or flat you live in? (pp. 24, 28)	
36	Can you say what number of rooms it has and where they are? (pp. 24, 28)	
37	Can you describe your bedroom and what you think of it? (pp. 24, 28–29)	
38	Can you say where you live, and where that is? (pp. 24, 30)	
39	Can you name ten places in your town or village? (p. 30)	
40	Can you describe your town or village? (pp. 24, 30–31)	
41	Can you talk about the good and the bad things about it? (pp. 30–31)	

Tourism and weather (pp. 25, 32–33, 34–35)

42	Can you ask for items in the Tourist Office? (pp. 25, 32–33)	
43	Can you help a Spanish visitor in the Tourist Office? (pp. 32–33)	
44	Can you ask and give information about tourist facilities? (pp. 25, 32–33)	
45	Can you describe what there is to do in an area? (pp. 25, 32–33)	
46	Can you say what the weather is like? (pp. 25, 34)	
47	Can you describe the main types of weather? (pp. 25, 34)	
48	Can you talk about the climate of an area? (p. 35)	
49	Can you name and locate six areas of Spain? (p. 35)	

Finding the way (pp. 36, 38–39)

50	Can you ask how to get to different places? (pp. 36, 38–39)	
51	Can you ask if there's a (chemist's) near here? (pp. 36, 38–39)	
52	Can you give directions? (pp. 36, 38–39)	
53	Can you explain exactly where a place is? (pp. 36, 38–39)	
54	Can you name types of streets and public buildings? (pp. 36, 38–39)	

Travel and transport (pp. 36, 40–41)

55	Can you understand simple signs and notices in the street? (p. 40)	
56	Can you buy different types of train and bus tickets? (p. 25)	
57	Can you ask for a book of bus tickets? (p. 25)	
58	Can you say and ask when trains or buses arrive and depart? (p. 25)	
59	Can you give the name of the Spanish rail company? (p. 40)	
60	Can you ask what platform the train leaves from? (p. 25)	
61	Can you ask for a smoking/non-smoking compartment? (p. 25)	
62	Can you name six different means of transport? (p. 41)?	
63	Can you say how you travel to school? (p. 41)	
64	Can you talk about how long it takes to get to school? (p. 41)	
65	Can you use adjectives to describe journeys and travel? (p. 41)	
66	Can you talk about the pros and cons of different types of travel? (p. 41)	

The environment (pp. 36, 42–43)

67	Can you say what we should do to protect the environment? (pp. 36, 42)	
68	Can you express what we should not do? (pp. 36, 42)	
69	Can you name six items which we should save, recycle or cut down on? (pp. 36, 42)	
70	Can you give the Spanish for ten verbs which show what we do to the environment (e.g. to consume - consumir)? (pp. 36, 42)	
71	Can you name six items related to pollution, traffic and oil? (pp. 36, 42)	
72	Can you explain your opinion using three different phrases? (p. 42)	
73	Can you say we should use less, more, not so much/many …? (p. 42)	
74	Can you describe the negative effects of what we do (e.g. it's harmful)? (pp. 36, 42).	
75	Can you describe the problems caused by cars? (p. 43)	
76	Can you say how the environment of your town could be improved? (pp. 36, 43)	
77	Can you say what you're worried about, environmentally? (pp. 36, 42)	

Topic checker

Leisure, going out (pp. 47, 50–51)

78	Can you ask what's on TV or at the cinema? (p. 47)	
79	Can you name six different types of films or programmes? (p. 47)	
80	Can you give your opinions on types of films and programmes? (pp. 47, 51)	
81	Can you name types or places of entertainment? (p. 47)	
82	Can you ask how much tickets cost? (p. 47)	
83	Can you find out where your seats are? (p. 47)	
84	Can you ask when an event starts and finishes? (p. 47)	
85	Can you invite someone out? (p. 51)	
86	Can you describe a film or programme you saw and give your opinion? (pp. 45, 51)	

Popular culture (pp. 52–53)

87	Can you talk about the type of clothes you like/don't like wearing? (pp. 46, 53)	
88	Can you give your views on fashion? (p. 53)	
89	Can you name different types of media? (p. 52)	
90	Can you give your opinion on the media? (p. 52)	
91	Can you talk about the media's role in promoting celebrities? (p. 52)	

Shopping (pp. 46, 54–55)

92	Can you ask where you can buy an item? (p. 46)	
93	Can you say what you'd like, ask if they have ...? (p. 46)	
94	Can you say you have no change, or you only have a 10-euro note? (p. 46)	
95	Can you say what size you take in clothes and shoes? (p. 46)	
96	Can you explain what the problem is with an item? (pp. 46, 54)	
97	Can you name ten items of clothing? (p. 46)	
98	Can you buy a present or gift? (pp. 46, 54)	
99	Can you understand a store guide? (p. 55)	

Accommodation and holidays (pp. 48, 56–58, 60–61)

100 Can you reserve different types of rooms? (pp. 58, 60)

101 Can you say for how many people and nights? (pp. 58, 60)

102 Can you act as receptionist as well as tourist? (pp. 58, 60)

103 Can you ask about mealtimes? (p. 58)

104 Can you ask about Internet facilities? (p. 59)

105 Can you explain that something is missing or not working? (p. 58)

106 Can you ask if there's room for a tent? (p. 58)

107 Can you write a letter of complaint? (pp. 58, 61)

108 Can you describe where you go on holiday, and what you usually do? (p. 56)

109 Can you describe a past holiday: where you went, what you did? (pp. 48, 56)

Restaurants (pp. 47, 57)

110 Can you explain what you would like for each course? (pp. 47, 57)

111 Can you ask what there is for vegetarians? (p. 47)

112 Can you say that you'd like to pay, please? (p. 47)

113 Can you complain that something is dirty or missing? (p. 47)

114 Can you check if the service charge is included? (p. 47)

Services and problems (pp. 62–63)

115 Can you name the parts of the body? (p. 62)

116 Can you explain that you don't feel well, and what's the matter? (p. 62)

117 Can you say how long you've been feeling ill? (p. 62)

118 Can you explain that you've lost something and describe it? (p. 63)

Staying in touch (pp. 58, 64–65)

119 Can you answer the phone and ask to speak to someone? (pp. 58, 64)

120 Can you explain that the line is engaged or that no one is answering? (pp. 58, 64)

121 Can you ask if you can leave a message? (pp. 58, 64)

122 Can you give the Spanish for a phone book, and a mobile phone? (pp. 58, 65)

123 Can you talk about the pros and cons of mobile phones? (p. 65)

Topic checker

Topic checker

School subjects, likes and dislikes (pp. 68–69, 72–73)

124	Can you say how many subjects you study, and what they are? (pp. 68, 72)	☐
125	Can you explain which subjects you like, and why? (pp. 68, 72)	☐
126	Can you name the subjects you don't like, and give a reason? (pp. 68, 72).	☐
127	Can you describe your school, and say what facilities it has? (pp. 69, 72)	☐
128	Can you describe your routine on a school day? (pp. 68–69, 72)	☐
129	Can you say what kind of marks you get? (pp. 69, 72)	☐
130	Can you give six adjectives for describing classmates, teachers and schools? (p. 68)	☐
131	Can you use ten verbs to describe activities at school? (p. 68)	☐
132	Can you give six nouns associated with good/bad behaviour? (p. 69)	☐

Part-time jobs (pp. 69, 74–75)

133	Can you say if you have a job and what you do? (pp. 69, 74)	☐
134	Can you describe your hours, and start and finish times? (pp. 69, 74)	☐
135	Can you say how much you earn? (pp. 69, 74)	☐
136	Can you give your opinion of your job? (pp. 69, 74–75)	☐
137	Can you ask others about their jobs, hours, earnings and opinions? (pp. 69, 74)	☐
138	Can you say what you spend your money on? (p. 75)	☐

Education issues (pp. 69, 76–77)

139	Can you give your opinion on school rules? (p. 76)	☐
140	Can you say what you think of school uniform? (p. 76)	☐
141	Can you describe the advantages of going to school? (p. 76)	☐
142	Can you explain what you think of discipline in your school? (p. 76)	☐
143	Can you say what you want to do next year? (p. 77)	☐
144	Can you say where you hope to go afterwards? (p. 77)	☐

Work experience (pp. 78, 80–81)

145 Can you explain where your did your work experience? (pp. 78, 80–81)

146 Can you describe how long it lasted? (pp. 78, 80–81)

147 Can you talk about your journey to and from work? (pp. 78, 80–81)

148 Can you give details of the hours you did? (pp. 78, 80–81)

149 Can you describe the work you had to do? (pp. 78, 80–81)

150 Can you say what you thought of your experience? (pp. 78, 80–81)

151 Can you talk about the pros and cons of work experience? (pp. 78, 80–81)

152 Can you use past and future tenses together? (pp. 27, 48, 59, 70–71, 81)

Future work and job applications (pp. 78, 82–85)

153 Can you explain what jobs your parent(s) or carer(s) do(es)? (p. 78)

154 Can you name eight different jobs or careers? (p. 78)

155 Can you understand the information on a CV? (p. 82)

156 Can you say which kind of work you would like to do? (pp. 78, 83)

157 Can you give a reason for your choice? (pp. 78, 83)

158 Can you say that you don't want to decide yet? (pp. 78, 83)

159 Can you explain that you will have to get a loan or a grant? (pp. 78, 83)

160 Can you understand job adverts? (p. 83)

161 Can you ask someone else about his/her future plans? (p. 78)

162 Can you talk about your own plans for study and work? (pp. 84–85)

163 Can you write a letter of application for a job? (p. 85)

Social concerns (pp. 86–87)

164 Can you say what causes you concern for the future? (pp. 86–87)

165 Can you identify attitudes and emotions? (pp. 86–87)

166 Can you say what you think the greatest social problems are? (pp. 86–87)

167 Can you explain who, in your opinion, we need to help? (pp. 86–87)

Topic checker

Vocabulary

A Personal information

¿Cómo te llamas? Me llamo …	*What's your name? I'm called …*
Mi nombre/apellido es …	*My first name/surname is …*
¿Cuántos años tienes? Tengo … años.	*How old are you? I'm … years old.*
¿Cuándo es tu cumpleaños?	*When is your birthday?*
Es el (primero/uno) (dos/tres) de mayo.	*It's the (first) (second/third) of May.*
¿De qué nacionalidad eres?	*What nationality are you?*
Soy (galés/galesa, inglés/inglesa).	*I'm (Welsh, English).*

remember >>

For the second or third of the month, simply use *el dos*, *el tres*.

a	*(ah)*	g	*(hay)*	m	*(emay)*	r	*(erray)*	x	*(aykees)*
b	*(bay)*	h	*(atch-ay)*	n	*(enay)*	s	*(essay)*	y	*(ee gree ay ga)*
c	*(thay)*	i	*(ee)*	ñ	*(enyay)*	t	*(tay)*	z	*(thay ta)*
d	*(day)*	j	*(hotta)*	o	*(oh)*	u	*(oo)*		¿Cómo se escribe …
e	*(ay)*	k	*(ka)*	p	*(pay)*	v	*(oovay)*		Se escribe …
f	*(effay)*	l	*(elay)*	q	*(coo)*	w	*(oovay doblay)*		¿Cómo se deletrea …

B Family and friends

¿Cuántas personas hay en tu familia?	*How many people are in your family?*
Somos (cinco). ¿Quiénes son?	*There are (five) of us. Who are they?*
Mis padres están separados/divorciados.	*My parents are separated/divorced.*
soltero/a, casado/a, viudo/a.	*single, married, a widower/widow*
¿Tienes hermanos?	*Have you got brothers and sisters?*
Sí, tengo … Soy hijo único/hija única.	*Yes, I have … I'm an only son/daughter.*

remember >>

With *soltero/a*, *casado/a*, *viudo/a* use the verb *ser*, e.g. *Es soltero*. (He is single.)

el hombre	*man*	el/la hermano/a	*brother/sister*	el/la primo/a	*cousin*
la mujer	*woman*	el hermanastro	*stepbrother*	el chico/la chica	*boy/girl*
el matrimonio	*married couple*	la hermanastra	*stepsister*	el/la adolescente	*teenager*
la pareja	*couple*	el/la gemelo/a	*twin*	el/la anciano/a	*elderly person*
la familia adoptiva	*adoptive family*	el/la huérfano/a	*orphan*	el/la extranjero/a	*foreigner*
el marido/esposo	*husband*	los padres	*parents*	el/la inmigrante	*immigrant*
la mujer/esposa	*wife*	los parientes	*relatives*	el/la vecino/a	*neighbour*
la madre soltera	*single mother*	el abuelo	*grandfather*	el/la amigo/a	*friend*
la madre, el padre	*mother, father*	la abuela	*grandmother*	el novio	*boyfriend*
la madrastra	*stepmother*	el/la tío/a	*uncle/aunt*	la novia	*girlfriend*
el padrastro	*stepfather*	el/la sobrino/a	*nephew/niece*	la juventud	*youth*

el estado civil	*marital status*	divorciarse	*to get divorced*	separarse	*to separate*
la boda	*wedding*	el divorcio	*divorce*	inmigrar	*to immigrate*
casarse	*to get married*	enamorarse	*to fall in love*	nacer	*to be born*
el casamiento	*marriage*	jubilarse	*to retire*	parecerse a	*to look like*

C Character

¿Cómo es tu carácter? Soy ...	What is your personality like? I'm ...
¿Cómo es tu (padre/madre)?	What's your (father/mother) like?
¿Cuáles son las características de ...	What are the characteristics of ...
un bueno amigo/una buena amiga?	a good friend?
Él/ella debe ser ...	He/she should be ...

afable	pleasant	gracioso/a	funny, witty
amistoso/a	friendly	hablador/a	talkative
atento/a	polite, attentive	honrado/a	honest
atrevido/a	daring, bold	introvertido/a	introverted
cariñoso/a	affectionate	maleducado/a	rude
celoso/a	jealous	mentiroso/a	liar
chistoso/a	jokey, funny	mezquino/a	mean, stingy
cobarde	cowardly	orgulloso/a	proud
comprensivo/a	understanding	perezoso/a	lazy
cortés	polite	seguro/a de sí mismo/a	confident
cuidadoso/a	careful	sensible	sensitive
egoísta	selfish, egotistic(al)	sensato/a	sensible
emprendedor/a	enterprising	serio/a	serious
encantador/a	charming, delightful	torpe	clumsy
extrovertido/a	extrovert, outgoing	travieso/a	naughty
formal	reliable, serious	valiente	brave

D Relationships

¿Te llevas bien con (tu hermano)?	Do you get on well with (your brother)?
Me llevo bien con .../no me llevo bien con ...	I get on well with .../I don't get on well with ...
Mi (hermana) me irrita, me fastidia,	My (sister) irritates me, annoys me,
me hace subirme por las paredes,	drives me up the wall,
me pone malo/a, me vuelve loco/a.	makes me ill, makes me mad/angry.
Me enfado con él, ella, mi (hermana).	I get angry with him, her, my (sister).
Su comportamiento/conducta es bueno/a, malo/a.	His/her behaviour is good/bad.
Las relaciones son buenas/malas.	Relations are good/bad.

normalmente	usually	discusiones	arguments	la barrera generacional	the generation gap
a veces	sometimes	estar de ...	to be in a ...	la cualidad	the quality
en general	generally	buen humor	good mood	el defecto	the defect
tener confianza (en)	to trust	mal humor	bad mood	la reacción	reaction
estar orgulloso/a (de)	to be proud (of)	enamorado/a	in love	la personalidad	personality
el sentido común	common sense	decepcionado/a	disappointed	pelearse con	to fight with

Grammar

A Nouns and articles

A noun can be a thing (e.g. *a bike*), a place (e.g. *a room*) or a person (e.g. *a man*).
A Spanish noun is either masculine (*m*) or feminine (*f*).
Nouns can be singular (*s*) (one of them) or plural (*pl*) (more than one).

The words for 'the', 'a' and 'some' are as follows:

	masculine	feminine		masculine	feminine
(s)	**un** chico	**una** chica	(s)	**el** hermano	**la** hermana
	a boy	*a girl*		*the brother*	*the sister*
(pl)	**unos** chicos	**unas** chicas	(pl)	**los** hermanos	**las** hermanas
	some boys	*some girls*		*the brothers*	*the sisters*

B Plural nouns

Ending in a vowel (a, e, i, o, u), add an **-s** in the plural: see the examples above.
Ending in a consonant, add an **-es: ordenador** (computer) – **ordenador<u>es</u>**.
An accent on the final syllable in the singular disappears in the plural: **salón, sal<u>ones</u>**.
Words from other languages can also just add **-s: clubs, cómics, pósters (or pósteres)**.

Put the following nouns in brackets into the plural.

Ejemplo: cuatro dormitorios

a cuatro (dormitorio) **c** dos (balcón) **e** dos (garaje)
b dos (terraza) **d** tres (pasillo) **f** cuatro (televisor)

C Adjectives

Adjectives describe a noun, e.g. blue, tall, good-looking are all adjectives.
In Spanish, the ending of an adjective has to 'agree' with the noun it describes.
If the noun is feminine and/or plural, for example, so will the adjective be:

(ms)	(fs)	(mpl)	(fpl)	(ms)	(fs)	(mpl)	(fpl)
-o	-a	-os	-as	**-ol**	-ola	-oles	-olas
-a	-a	-as	-as	**-or**	-ora	-ores	-oras
-e	-e	-es	-es	**-án**	-ana	-anes	-anas
-és	-esa	-eses	-esas				

Other consonants: no change in (*fs*), add **-es** for both (*mpl*) and (*fpl*).
Marrón (*brown*), **cortés** (*polite*), **mayor/menor** (*older/younger*): no change in the (*fs*).
Lila (*lilac*), **naranja** (*orange*) and **rosa** (*pink*) may add an **-s** in the plural, (e.g. **calcetines naranja or calcetines naranjas**).

Write the correct form of the adjective in Ana's description of herself and her family.

Ejemplo: Yo soy baja y de estatura mediana ...

Yo soy (bajo) y de estatura mediana, pero mi hermana (mayor) es (alto) y (delgado). Tengo los ojos (verde) y el pelo (castaño) y soy (educado) y bastante (callado). Sin embargo, ella es (impaciente) y (hablador). ¿Mis hermanos (menor)? Son (inteligente) y (gracioso).

D Regular present verbs

Spanish verbs end in **-ar**, **-er**, **-ir** in the infinitive form. The infinitive is the verb form which means 'to ...' in English: e.g. **hablar** means <u>to</u> speak, **comer** <u>to</u> eat, and **vivir** <u>to</u> live.

Below is the regular present tense. The present tense indicates what usually happens, or what happens at the moment, e.g. I go to school, I eat lunch at one, I live in Sheffield.

	hablar *(to speak)*	comer *(to eat)*	vivir *(to live)*
yo	habl**o**	com**o**	viv**o**
tú	habl**as**	com**es**	viv**es**
él, ella, usted	habl**a**	com**e**	viv**e**
nosotros/as	habl**amos**	com**emos**	viv**imos**
vosotros/as	habl**áis**	com**éis**	viv**ís**
ellos, ellas, ustedes	habl**an**	com**en**	viv**en**

E Irregular present tense verbs

These common verbs are only irregular in the **yo** (*I*) form.

dar *(to give)*	**doy**	saber *(to know how to/a fact)*	**sé**
conocer *(to know a person/place)*	**conozco**	salir *(to go out, leave)*	**salgo**
hacer *(to do, make)*	**hago**	traer *(to bring)*	**traigo**
poner *(to put, set, lay)*	**pongo**	ver *(to see)*	**veo***

* Ver keeps an 'e' before the endings: ve**o**, ve**s**, ve, ve**mos**, ve**is**, ve**n**

These common verbs are irregular. The six parts of each are as follows:
ir *(to go)* voy, vas, va, vamos, vais, van
estar *(to be)* estoy, estás, está, estamos, estáis, están
ser *(to be)* soy, eres, es, somos, sois, son
tener *(to have)* tengo, tienes, tiene, tenemos, tenéis, tienen

Write each verb in the dialogue below in its correct form. **Ejemplo:** 1 – conoces

1 Marta, ¿(conocer) a mi amiga Sharon? — Encantada. ¿De dónde (ser), Sharon?
2 Yo (vivir) en Edimburgo, en Escocia. — Sharon, ¿qué (hacer) aquí en España?
3 Mi hermano y yo (estar) de vacaciones. — ¿Cuántos años (tener) tu hermano?
4 Dieciocho años – y ¡(ser) muy guapo! — Y vosotros, ¿adónde (ir) esta tarde?
5 Yo no lo (saber) todavía. ¿Por qué? — Nosotros (salir) pronto. ¿Queréis venir al club?

F Reflexive verbs

Reflexive verbs indicate an action done to oneself. They have a pronoun (**me**, **te**, etc.) in front.

yo	**me lavo**	*I wash*	nosotros/as	**nos lavamos**	*we wash*
tú	**te lavas**	*you wash*	vosotros/as	**os laváis**	*you wash*
él	**se lava**	*he washes*	ellos	**se lavan**	*they wash*
ella	**se lava**	*she washes*	ellas	**se lavan**	*they wash*
usted	**se lava**	*you wash*	ustedes	**se lavan**	*you wash*

Self, family and friends

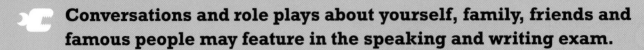

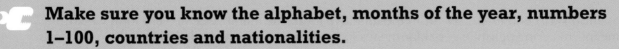

- Conversations and role plays about yourself, family, friends and famous people may feature in the speaking and writing exam.

- Make sure you know the alphabet, months of the year, numbers 1–100, countries and nationalities.

A Personal details

SPEAK

1. You need to be able to exchange personal information and details with others.

2. Read the conversation below. Study the IT club register.

Cambia las palabras en negrita. Inventa cuatro conversaciones más. *Change the words in bold. Invent four more conversations.*

- – ¿Cómo te llamas?
- + Me llamo **Marta**.
- – ¿Cuál es tu apellido?
- + Es **Duarte**.
- – ¿Cómo se escribe?
- + **D-U-A-R-T-E**.
- – ¿Cuántos años tienes?
- + Tengo **quince** años.
- – ¿Cuándo es tu cumpleaños?
- + Es el **uno de febrero**.

Club de Informática

	Apellido	Nombre	Edad	Cumpleaños
1	Duarte	Marta	15	1/2
2	Elizalde	Curro	14	29/8
3	Gallego	Javier	17	15/4
4	Moreno	Zohora	13	20/7
5	Tejero	Nuria	16	3/11

B Describing yourself and others

WRITE

1. You may be asked to describe your build, hair and eyes. Use the dictionary to look up any words below which you don't know.

2. **¿Cómo eres? Describe tu físico.** *Describe what you look like.*

(Height)	Soy	alto(a)/bajo(a)/de estatura mediana.
(Shape)		delgado(a)/fuerte/gordito(a).
(Hair colour)		castaño/rubio/negro.
(Hair length)	Tengo el pelo	corto/largo/hasta los hombros.
(Hair texture)		rizado/liso/ondulado.
(Eyes)	Tengo los ojos	marrones/verdes/grises/azules.
(Other features)	Llevo	gafas/lentillas/barba/bigote.

study hint >>

When describing someone else, you'll need the verbs *es, tiene, lleva*.

C Family and friends

In the next activity, you have to match the paragraphs A–G of the letter to the correct topics. There will be one left over. Look for the words you know. What clues do they give you?

Escribe la letra en cada casilla. No se necesitan todas las letras. *Write the letter in each box. You do not need all the letters.*

1 Name ☐

2 Age ☐

3 Birthday ☐

4 Nationality ☐

5 Brothers/sisters ☐

6 Parents ☐

A Su cumpleaños es el doce de junio.

B Le gustan mucho los animales, y tiene un perro negro y marrón – ¡dice que es su mejor amigo!

C Mi compañero de clase se llama Iñigo Bernal Arroyos.

D Su padre no vive con su madre – están separados.

E Tiene una hermana menor, Nieves, pero no tiene hermanos.

F Es colombiano. Nació aqui en la capital, Bogotá.

G Tiene dieciséis años, y vive con su familia en las afueras de la cuidad.

>> practice questions

As part of the assessed speaking task, you may be asked to describe someone you know or admire. Use the notes below to speak about an online Spanish friend you have made.

1	Nombre y Apellido:	Ana Gómez
2	Nacionalidad:	española
3	Lugar de nacimiento:	Granada
4	Fecha de nacimiento:	23–7–1988
5	Familia:	un hermano (Pablo), padres divorciados
6	Animales:	gato (gris, blanco)

exam tip >>

You will need to use verbs in the third person (*él/ella*). You can find them in Activity C above.

Daily routine

🔌 **Describe your routine during the week, and at weekends.**

🔌 **Talk or write about what you do to help at home.**

A Daily routine

>> **key fact** **Reflexive verbs are very important here:** *me levanto,*
me visto ..., etc.

① Make sure you revise question words thoroughly:

¿cuando? (when?); **¿quién?** (who?); **¿dónde?** (where?); **¿qué?** (what?); **¿cómo?** (how?); **¿cuál?** (which?);
¿por qué? (why?); **¿adónde?** (where ... to?); **¿cuánto?** (how much?); **¿a qué hora?** (at what time?).

② Read the questions below and work out the appropriate question word in Spanish for
numbers 1, 3, 5, 7, 9, 11, 13, 15.

③ Answer each question so it is true for you. Begin each answer with the verb in brackets.

Contesta a estas preguntas en español. *Answer these questions in Spanish.*

1	¿(*At what time*) te levantas?	(Me levanto ...)
2	¿Qué llevas para ir al instituto?	(Llevo ...)
3	¿(*How*) vas al instituto?	(Voy ...)
4	¿A qué hora sales de casa?	(Salgo ...)
5	¿(*How much*) tiempo tardas en llegar?	(Tardo ...)
6	¿A qué hora empiezan las clases?	(Empiezan ...)
7	¿(*How many*) clases hay al día?	(Hay ...)
8	¿Cuánto tiempo duran las clases?	(Las clases duran ...)
9	¿(*When*) hay recreos?	(Hay recreos ...)
10	¿A qué hora terminan las clases?	(Terminan ...)
11	¿(*Where*) comes al mediodía?	(Como ...)
12	¿Cuándo vuelves a casa?	(Vuelvo ...)
13	¿(*How many*) horas de deberes haces?	(Hago ...)
14	¿Qué te gusta hacer por la tarde?	(Me gusta ...)
15	¿(*At what time*) te acuestas?	(Me acuesto a ...)

④ Rewrite the Spanish verbs in brackets above to talk about the routine of a Spanish-speaking teenager.
Look back to the verb tables on page 5. (You may not need to change all the verbs.)

Ejemplo: (Me levanto) – se levanta.

⑤ How is your routine different at the weekend? Write a paragraph explaining when you get up, what
you do during the day, and when you go to bed. Look at 'Interests and Hobbies' on pages 14–15.

B Helping at home

To express having to do something, use verbs of obligation: *tener que* (to have to), *deber* (ought to, must), and *hay que* (one has to).

READ

1. Read the verbs in the list below, on the right. They will be useful in describing what you do to help at home. Can you give the English for each?

2. Choose the correct verb for each gap in the conversation. You can use some more than once.

–	¿Tienes que ayudar en casa?	cortar
+	Sí. Mi madre es soltera, y dice que todo el mundo debe ... **(1)** ... porque ella no puede hacerlo todo.	recoger
–	¿Qué tienes que hacer?	limpiar
+	Todos los días, tengo que ... **(2)** ... la cama, ... **(3)** ... mi dormitorio, ... **(4)** ... al perro por la mañana, y a veces ayudo a ... **(5)** ... la cena.	lavar
+	¿Qué tienen que hacer tus hermanos?	preparar
–	Mi hermana mayor, que tiene diecinueve años, ayuda por la tarde. Entre semana, suele ... **(6)** ... el suelo de la cocina, ... **(7)** ... la aspiradora y planchar.	barrer
+	¿Y tu hermano menor?	pasar
-	Mi hermano debe ... **(8)**. ... o ... **(9)** ... la mesa, pero es muy vago. El fin de semana, le gusta ayudar a ... **(10)** ... el coche.	poner
+	¿Quién suele ... **(11)** ... los platos?	ayudar
-	Nadie, porque tenemos lavaplatos – ¡afortunadamente!	regar
+	Y tu madre – ¿qué hace ella?	quitar
-	Trabaja mucho, pero suele cocinar, ... **(12)** ... la compra, ... **(13)** ... la ropa y ... **(14)** ... las plantas de la terraza. Los sábados por la mañana, hay que ... **(15)** ... la casa, y todo el mundo tiene que echar una mano.	sacar
+	¿Hay alguna tarea que no te guste?	hacer
-	Odio ... **(16)**... la basura, y en verano detesto ... **(17)** ... el césped porque es superaburrido. Sé que debo ayudar más, pero tengo muchos deberes.	fregar

3. Find the Spanish for the following expressions of time in the conversation above.

1	every day	3	during the week	5	in the evening	7	at the weekend
2	sometimes	4	in the morning	6	on Saturday mornings	8	in summer

>> practice questions

Prepare a similar conversation for you and a friend to use as part of your speaking assessment. Adapt the questions and replies from B. Don't forget to add in expressions of time, and your likes/dislikes.

study hint >>

Tengo que (I have to), *tiene que* (he/she has to), *debo* (I ought to), *debe* (he/she ought to), *hay que* (one has to) are followed by the infinitive (e.g. *planchar*).

Relationships

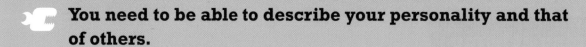

You need to be able to describe your personality and that of others.

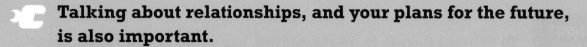

Talking about relationships, and your plans for the future, is also important.

A Personality, moods and feelings

>> **key fact** To describe character traits, Spanish uses the verb *ser* (to be). For moods and feelings, *estar* (to be) is used.

1 **Ser** and **estar** also appear in other contexts. Read the table below.

Both *ser* and *estar* mean 'to be', but are used in different contexts:

SER	ESTAR
Permanent characteristics E.g. Es simpático. (*He's nice.*)	**Temporary states** E.g. El té está caliente. (*The tea is hot.*)
Jobs, professions E.g. Soy enfermera. (*I'm a nurse.*)	**Feelings, moods** E.g. Estoy deprimido. (*I'm depressed.*)
Time E.g. Es la una. (*It's one o'clock.*)	**Position, place** E.g. Está a la izquierda. (*It's on the left.*)

READ

2 Does each sentence below need **ser** or **estar**? Choose the correct word in brackets.

(Puri) ¿Yo? (Soy/Estoy) una persona amable y educado. (Soy/Estoy) muy contenta con mi vida.

(Alisa) Mi madre (está, es) estresada porque mi abuelo no (es, está) muy bien.

(Diego) Mis amigos dicen que (soy/estoy) seguro de mí mismo y alegre.

(Luis) Mi padre (es/está) deprimido porque no tiene trabajo.

(Rafa) (Estoy/soy) ilusionado - voy a hacer un intercambio escolar.

(Miki) (Estoy/soy) enfadado con mi hermano. Dice que yo (soy/estoy) torpe, y no es verdad.

3 This exam-type task asks you to re-read the descriptions above and identify who is speaking in each sentence 1–9 below.

Escribe el nombre de la persona apropiada. *Write the name of the appropriate person.*

Who ...

1	is excited?	**4**	has a depressed family member?	**7**	is happy with life?
2	is confident?	**5**	is polite?	**8**	is cheerful?
3	is angry?	**6**	has a parent who is stressed?	**9**	denies being slow?

B Future relationships

>> **key fact**

You need to show you can read for overall meaning, as well as detail.

READ

 Read the young people's views on marriage in the magazine article below 'Casarte - ¿pro o contra?'. Watch for negatives which change the meaning: e.g. **nunca/jamás** (never), **nadie** (no-one).

La idea de un matrimonio feliz (como el de mis padres) me atrae, pero más tarde. De momento, prefiero dedicarme a estudiar, para luego montar mi propio negocio. *(Gabriel)*

¡Tengo muchas ganas! Lo tengo todo planeado ya: la boda, la iglesia, los invitados, la luna de miel, el traje de novia (claro) – ¡solo me falta el novio! *(Carlita)*

Como soy gay, 'casarme' puede ser difícil. No estoy seguro de si se permite el matrimonio entre personas del mismo sexo en mi país. Tal vez, una union civil. *(Miguel)*

No digo nunca, pero hay cosas que quiero hacer. Por un lado, quiero ir a la universidad, viajar al extranjero, y estoy entusiasmada ante las perspectivas de mi carrera (quiero ser abogada). Por otro lado, tener a alguien con quien compartir mi vida sería muy agradable. *(Rosa)*

Hay que ser maduro para vivir con otra persona. Mi madre se fue a vivir con mi padre a los diecisiete años y tuvo dos niños antes de los veinte. Su matrimonio duró poco, a causa de los problemas de mi padre con el alcohol y la violencia. No voy a arrejuntarme* con nadie hasta cerca de los treinta años. Tal vez, nunca. *(Andrés)*
*arrejuntarse – *to shack up with*

¿Hablas en serio? No me interesa perder el tiempo cuidando a un marido o estropear mi cuerpo con un embarazo* tras otro. Tener un novio, sí. Casarme, jamás. *(Tere)*
*embarazo – *pregnancy*

2 Escribe los nombres en las casillas correctas. *Write the names in the correct boxes.*

¿Casarme? Sí	¿Casarme? No	¿Casarme? No sé …

3 Now answer these questions in English. They test your ability to read for detail.

1 What does Gabriel want to do first? (2)

2 What is Miguel not sure about? (1)

3 Which features of a wedding does Carlita mention? Name three. (3)

4 What problems did Andrés' father have? (2)

5 Write down two things Rosa wants to do. (2)

6 Note two reasons Tere gives for her decision about marriage. (2)

>> practice questions

READ

Prepare a paragraph in reply to the questions: ¿Y tú? ¿Quieres casarte? ¿Por qué? ¿Por qué no? Use and adapt phrases from the article above.

Vocabulary

A Healthy living

¿Qué haces para estar sano/a, en forma?	*What do you do to be healthy, fit?*
¿Qué hay que hacer para ...	*What do you have to do in order to ...*
llevar una vida sana/mantenerse en forma?	*lead a healthy life/stay healthy?*
Hago ejercicio, duermo/como bien.	*I take exercise, I sleep/eat well.*
Hay que (beber menos alcohol).	*You have to (drink less alcohol).*
Se debe (dormir siete horas al día).	*You ought (to sleep for seven hours a day).*
Hace falta (respetar el cuerpo).	*It's necessary to (respect one's body).*
¿Qué deportes practicas?	*What sports do you play?*
Juego al fútbol/baloncesto/billar/voleibol.	*I play football/basketball/billiards/volleyball.*
Practico el atletismo/el piragüismo/ el alpinismo.	*I do athletics/canoeing/ mountain-climbing.*
Hago gimnasia/judo/aerobic/boxeo.	*I do gymnastics/judo/aerobics/boxing.*
Hago ciclismo/vela/footing/natación.	*I go cycling/sailing/jogging/swimming.*

> **remember >>**
>
> **Use *jugar* for playing ball games, and *tocar* for playing musical instruments.**

evitar, seguir	*to avoid, to follow*	puede resultar en	*(it) can result in*
utilizar, abusar, tomar	*use, abuse, take*	puede conducir a	*(it) can lead to*
fumar cigarrillos	*to smoke cigarettes*	problemas con	*problems with*
el tabaquismo	*tobacco addiction*	dificultades con	*difficulties with*
las drogas, drogarse	*drugs, to take drugs*	es dañino/a (para)	*it's harmful (to)*
emborracharse	*to get drunk*	es peligroso para	*it's dangerous for*
seropositivo, el SIDA	*HIV positive, AIDS*	el corazón, el hígado	*the heart, the liver*
estar a régimen	*to be on a diet*	el cerebro, la salud	*the brain, health*
una dieta sana	*a healthy diet*	los pulmones	*the lungs*

B The Internet

abrir, apagar	*to open, to shut down*	estar conectado/a	*to be online*
el archivo	*file*	guardar	*to save*
la banda ancha	*broadband*	el/la internauta	*Internet user*
el buscador	*search engine*	el ordenador	*computer*
borrar	*to delete*	el ordenador portátil	*laptop*
una cuenta, un perfil	*an account, a profile*	navegar en/por Internet	*to surf the Web*
chatear	*to chat*	la página web	*web page*
la contraseña	*password*	el ratón	*mouse*
el correo basura	*junk mail, spam*	la red	*network, Internet*
el correo electrónico	*email*	la sala de chat	*chat room*
el correo ordinario	*normal delivery*	el sitio web	*website*
un email, un emoticón	*an email, a smiley*	el teclado	*keyboard*
el disco duro	*hard disk*	el técnico	*technician*

Grammar

C Gustar (to like, be pleasing to)

Gustar means 'to be pleasing to', translated in English as 'to like'.

With singular nouns (**el, la**), use **gusta**. With plural nouns (**los, las**) use **gustan**.

Gustar can also be used with a verb in its infinitive form (i.e. ends in **-ar**, **-er**, **ir**)

Me gusta el inglés.	*I like English. (To me is pleasing English.)*
Me gusta la informática.	*I like IT. (To me is pleasing IT.)*
Me gustan los trabajos manuales.	*I like CDT. (To me is pleasing CDT.)*
Me gustan las matemáticas.	*I like maths. (To me is pleasing maths.)*
Me gusta tocar la guitarra.	*I like playing the guitar.*

The verb **encantar** (to delight), **interesar** (to interest), **importar** (to matter) behave in the same way as **gustar**. Before **gustar** and similar verbs, you need an indirect object pronoun.

D Indirect object pronouns

(yo)	**me**	*to me*	(nosotros/as)	**nos**	*to us*
(tú)	**te**	*to you*	(vosotros/as)	**os**	*to you*
(él, ella, usted)	**le**	*to him, her, you*	(ellos, ellas, ustedes)	**les**	*to them, to you*

¿Te gusta el fútbol? No me interesa.	*Do you like fotball? I'm not interested in it.*
A Felipe le encanta la equitación.	*Felipe loves horse-riding.*
¡No nos gusta el deporte!	*We don't like sport!*
Me importa mucho la salud.	*(My) health matters to me/is important.*

E Se

Using **se** with the third person singular of the verb is equivalent in English to *one ...*, *they ...*, *people ...*, *you/we ...* . It indicates what generally happens or is done:

En España, se bebe más café.	*In Spain, they drink more coffee.*
Se come menos grasa animal.	*People eat less animal fat.*
Se hace más ejercicio en verano.	*One does more exercise in summer.*
Aquí se habla inglés.	*English is spoken here.*

When the item following the verb is plural, you need the third person plural of the verb (**ellos/ellas/ustedes**):

¿Se venden sombreros de paja?	*Do you sell straw hats here?*
Se comen más patatas en Gran Bretaña.	*They/we eat more potatoes in Great Britain.*
Se hablan catalán y castellano en Cataluña.	*Catalan and Spanish are spoken in Cataluña.*

Put the verbs in brackets into the correct form, using **se**. **Ejemplo:** En España, se bebe más café que té ...

En España, (beber) más café que té y (comer) más verduras y fruta que aquí en Gran Bretaña. (Tomar) menos grasa animal también pero (fumar) más cigarrillos en los lugares públicos. No (tomar) tantos dulces, aunque el turrón que (fabricar) cerca de Alicante es muy popular en Navidad.

Interests and hobbies

 You need to be able to talk about sports, hobbies and interests.

 Giving your opinion and expressing your likes and dislikes is also important.

A Likes and dislikes

WRITE

Read the phrases below, and study the table of hobbies and symbols. Write a sentence for each young person using as many different expressions of liking/disliking as you can, e.g. **Merche: Me gusta el alpinismo y me encanta jugar al rugby, pero odio hacer natación.**

study hint >>

Learn a variety of ways of saying what you like or don't like.

me gusta (mucho)	*I like (a lot)*	no me gusta nada	*I don't like at all*
me encanta*, prefiero	*I love, I prefer*	odio/detesto	*I hate*
me interesa*	*I'm interested in*	no aguanto	*I can't stand*
me da* igual	*I don't mind*	me fastidia*	*(it) annoys me*
me fascina*	*I find ... fascinating*	no me atrae*	*(it) doesn't appeal*

* These verbs follow the same pattern as **gustar**.

	♥	♥ ♥	✗ ✗
Merche	el alpinismo	el rugby	la natación
Felipe	el piragüismo	el footing	el golf
Raúl	el hockey	el voleibol	la equitación
Cisco	las cartas	el ajedrez	el deporte

B Giving reasons

WRITE

Write these Spanish words with their English equivalents (using the dictionary if necessary) in two columns as indicated below.

study hint >>

Make sure you can say why you like or dislike a sport or hobby.

barato/a	estúpido/a	caro/a
divertido/a	relajante	duro/a
aburrido/a	emocionante	fácil
peligroso/a	fascinante	gratis
entretenido/a	genial	inútil

☺	☹
barato/a - cheap	caro/a -

C The Internet

>> **key fact** You need to be familiar with the language of computers and the Internet.

READ

1 Contesta a las preguntas en inglés.
Answer the questions in English.

1 What does Marta think of computers?
2 What kind of computer does she have?
3 Note two problems she has.
4 What does she get irritated about?
5 Where does she go after school?
6 Write down two things she does there.
7 What is Tuenti?
8 Which two things does she ask?

> ¡A mí me encantan los ordenadores! Desafortunadamente, el disco duro de mi ordenador portátil no es muy grande. Además, no tenemos banda ancha aquí, así que no puedo descargar archivos grandes. Y recibo mucho correo basura - ¡me molesta mucho! Después de las clases, me gusta ir al cibercafé y navegar por Internet. A veces, leo páginas de sitios webs británicos, o paso quince minutos en salas de chat con otros internautas. Tengo un perfil en Tuenti, que es una red social española como Facebook: ¿tienes tú una cuenta? ¿Quieres invitarme a ser tu amiga? ¡Hasta pronto! Marta

2 Use Marta's email to write a paragraph about your own use of the computer and the Internet.

D Saying when and how often

>> **key fact** Earn more marks by adding detail about when and how often.

WRITE

Escribe en español las frases en inglés. *Write the English phrases in Spanish.*

1 en primavera (in spring)   *in summer, in autumn, in winter*
2 una vez a la semana (once a week)   *once a month*
3 dos veces por semana (twice a week) *three times a week*
4 los viernes a la noche (on Friday nights) *on Monday nights*
5 los jueves/domingos (on Thursdays/Sundays) *on Tuesdays/Saturdays*

>> practice questions

SPEAK

Practise the following conversation. Then answer the four questions, so that they are true for you, in Spanish.

– ¿Qué te gusta hacer en tu tiempo libre?
+ …(1)… me gusta jugar al baloncesto. Juego al fútbol y practico la natación …(2)… .
– ¿Eres miembro de algún club?
+ Soy miembro del club de ordenadores. Nos reunimos ..(3)… .
– ¿Tocas algún instrumento?
+ El martes …(4)… tengo clase de guitarra.
– ¿Qué haces el fin de semana?
+ …(5)… voy con mis amigos a la discoteca. También hago mis deberes …(6)… .

1 in winter
2 in July and August
3 twice a week
4 after school
5 on Friday nights
6 on Sundays

Healthy living

- Learn to say what you do to stay healthy.

- Make sure you can give your opinion on health-related issues.

A Staying healthy

>> **key fact** Reading articles carefully builds your writing and speaking skills.

READ

First, read for general meaning. Study Joaquin's post on the school web.

¿De qué temas hablan Joaquín, Alicia y Paco? Escribe ✓ en las casillas correctas. *Which topics do Joaquín, Alicia and Paco mention? Write ✓ in the correct boxes.*

| A la comida | ☐ | C la bebida | ☐ | E no estar bien | ☐ | G las tareas | ☐ |
| B el ejercicio físico | ☐ | D el estrés | ☐ | F el tabaco | ☐ | H las drogas | ☐ |

Soy muy deportista. Hago footing dos veces a la semana, y voy a la piscina el sábado. No bebo alcohol – es malo para la salud. Muchos de mis amigos fuman, pero yo no. Sigo un régimen sano con mucha fruta y verdura.

Joaquín

Yo soy adicto al chocolate (dos tabletas al día), y a los cigarrillos – ocho o diez al día. Pero no tomo drogas. No hago nunca ejercicio. Todos los días me digo que voy a cambiar, pero no lo hago.

Paco

Me levanto temprano todos los días para hacer yoga, y voy a mi trabajo andando. Nunca uso el coche, por eso ¡no estoy nada estresada! Tomo un poco de vino con la cena cada noche, pero aparte de eso, no bebo.

Alicia

B Reading for detail

1. Read for detail. Take care with expressions of degree: **bastante** (quite a lot), **bien** (well), **muy** (very), **poco** (little).

2. **Para cada frase a–f, escribe el nombre de la persona apropiada.** *For each sentence a–f, write the name of the appropriate person.*

   a   Le gusta ir a pie.
   b   Fuma bastante.
   c   Hace ejercicio físico todos los días.
   d   Come bien.
   e   Bebe poco.
   f   Es muy perezoso/a.

C Health issues

1 Use these strategies to help you work out the meaning of unfamiliar words.

Say it aloud. Does it sound similar to an English word?	parque	*park*
Change **z** to **c** or **s**	comenzar	*commence*
Take off the final **o**, **a**, or **e**	económico	*economic*
Take off an **e** at the start of a word	especial	*special*
Take off a final **se**: it may be a reflexive verb	servirse	*to serve, use*

WRITE

2 Read the following words and write down their English meanings.

Verbs	abusar, atacar, utilizar, drogarse, inyectarse, provocar, relajarse
Nouns	el ataque, el alcoholismo, el drogadicto, el estrés, el fumador, el síndrome de abstinencia, el sistema, la sustancia, el tabaquismo, la vena
Adjectives	cardiaco/a, pasivo/a, químico/a, respiratorio/a, psicológico/a

remember >>

Suelo ..., followed by the infinitive, means 'to ... usually' (do something): e.g. *Suelo lavar los platos.* (I usually wash the dishes.)

>> key fact You can put together simple vocabulary to express more complex meanings.

3 Write the following in Spanish, using the words above and others you already know.

- a passive smoker, passive smoking, to inject oneself in a vein
- to provoke (induce/bring on) a heart attack or psychological stress
- to use chemical substances, to drug oneself up with dangerous substances
- to attack the respiratory system

>> practice questions

WRITE

Use the vocabulary section (page 12), the phrases above, the texts on page 16, and your dictionary to put together your own replies to these questions.

a ¿Qué haces tú para estar en forma?

b ¿Qué hay que hacer para llevar una vida sana?

c ¿Cuáles son los peligros de fumar, beber mucho, o tomar drogas?

remember >>

The phrases *es importante* (it's important), *es necesario/ hace falta* (it's necessary), *se debe* (one ought), *hay que* (one has to) can be used with *no* and the infinitive, e.g. *Es importante no fumar.*

Mealtimes and special occasions

- You need to understand and talk about special occasions.
- You also need to be able to discuss mealtimes and food preferences.

A Special occasions

1 Five teenagers talk about special occasions.

¿Quién habla de cada tema 1–8? Escribe ✗ en las 8 casillas correctas. *Who mentions each topic 1–8? Put a cross in the 8 correct boxes.*

exam tip >>

You may have to put ticks or crosses in a grid - read the question carefully to determine how many.

A Celebramos el cumpleaños de cada miembro de la familia, y el santo también.

B En Milad-an-Nabi se celebra la vida de Mahoma. Se lee el Corán, se recitan oraciones, se cantan canciones sagradas y vamos a la mezquita con mi abuelo. También se da comida y dinero a los pobres.

C Sí. En Nochebuena montamos el árbol de Navidad, decoramos la casa, nos vestimos de fiesta, y vamos a la Misa del Gallo en la iglesia, a medianoche.

D En Semana Santa hay procesiones por las calles, y pasos* con imágenes de Cristo, María y los discípulos.

E En cualquier fiesta siempre se prepara algo típico y vienen mis parientes a casa. Se sirven carnes, pescados, tartas y dulces … ¡Mucho trabajo!

* un paso – a float in a religious procession, carried through street.

	A	B	C	D	E
1 prayers and songs					
2 making special food					
3 giving to the poor					
4 celebrating your 'saint's day'					
5 relatives visiting the home					
6 getting dressed up					
7 street processions					
8 Christmas tree					

WRITE/SPEAK

2 Use and adapt the texts above to answer these questions: **¿Qué fiestas se celebran en tu familia? ¿Qué hacéis? ¿Se prepara comida especial para estas fiestas?**

1 You will need to explain when, where and with whom you have your meals.

¿Cada persona habla de la mañana (M), del mediodía (D) o de la tarde (T)? *Is each person talking about the morning (M), midday (D) or evening (T)?*

No tengo hambre. No desayuno mucho: cereales con leche y un café.

Dani ☐

Suelo tomar tostadas y un zumo de fruta. ¡No tengo mucho tiempo para desayunar más!

Paco ☐

El fin de semana comemos sobre la una y media: dos o tres platos y un postre.

Lorenzo ☐

A veces ceno delante de la tele con mi hermano, pero en general ceno con mi familia en el comedor.

Nuria ☐

Almuerzo en el instituto con mis amigos. Voy a la cafetería, y tomo un bocadillo o una pizza.

Alicia ☐

2 Which foods do you like or dislike, or not eat? Read Ben's account below, and find five expressions for liking, disliking, or preferring.

>> **key fact** **Learn as many ways of expressing likes and dislikes as you can. They will be useful in many different topic areas.**

>> practice questions

¡Hola, me llamo Ben! ¿Qué tipo de comida me gusta? Pues, ¡muchas cosas! Me gustan las pastas – macarrones, espaguetis, lasaña con salsa de tomate y queso. Sin embargo, no tomo ni pescado ni carne. Me encantan los huevos también, pero lo que más me gusta es la tortilla española. Además, las verduras y las ensaladas son muy buenas. Pero odio la colifor: es algo que no aguanto. En cuanto a bebidas, prefiero el zumo de fruta – pero no bebo café.

Read Ben's description again, and complete the form.

Nombre: ....

Comida preferida: ....

Detesta: ....

Le gusta beber: ....

¿Vegetariano/a? (dibuja un círculo) Sí/No

exam tip >>

Read forms carefully in the exam, and write down only the information you're asked for. Here for example, *comida preferida* means the food he prefers above all others, not just any foods he likes.

New technology

- You need to say how you use new technologies.

- You will need to understand and talk about the advantages and disadvantages.

A Using technology

>> **key fact**   Many words related to technology are similar to English ones.

READ

Lee los correos electrónicos. Para cada persona, escribe la letra del dibujo apropiado. *Read the emails: for each person write the letter of the appropriate picture below.*

TÚ Y LAS TECNOLOGÍAS MODERNAS

¿Cómo te aprovechas?
¡Mándanos un correo electrónico!

Yo uso mi teléfono móvil todo el tiempo. ¡No me puedo imaginar la vida sin móviles! *(Ricardo)*

Debido* a la invención de nuevos materiales, tengo una silla de ruedas muy ligera, pero muy fuerte. Me encanta el deporte y un día quiero representar a mi país en los Juegos Paralímpicos. *(Carmen)*

Uso Internet todos los días para aprender, informarme* y divertirme. *(Susi)*

¡Qué bien la invención de ese 'freeware'! ¡Me permite hacer llamadas telefónicas por Internet gratis! *(Pablo)*

Mi hermano usa mucho su agenda electrónica para acceder a Internet, hacer llamadas telefónicas, ver videoclips – es como una oficina portátil. Es superguay ... ¡Quiero una! *(Alicia)*

Yo vivo con el cáncer desde la edad de tres años. Voy a la clínica regularmente para seguir mis tratamientos. La vida va a cambiar más de lo imaginable, gracias a los avances en la bio y nanotecnología. *(Gabi)*

*debido - *due to, owing to*
*informarse - *get information, find out about*

Ricardo ☐

Carmen ☐

Susi ☐

Pablo ☐

Alicia ☐

Gabi ☐

exam tip >>

There may be unfamiliar language in the exam, but you will be given an English translation if they are important to understand.

B New technologies – for and against

Use chunks of simple language to build more complex phrases.

READD

1 Read the grid of phrases below and use the strategies from page 17 to work out the meanings before looking them up in the dictionary.

lo bueno/malo, la (des)ventaja, el problema, el peligro de Internet, de la red, del ciberespacio, de las nuevas tecnologías	es que ...
es posible puedes	ponerte/estar/mantenerte en contacto con ..., hacer amigos, conocer a gente tener mucha información a mano, compartir información y fotos con ... mantenerte al corriente (de las noticias/lo que pasa, de un hobby) encontrar muchos puntos de vista/ aprender mucho (sobre ...) ver/escuchar programas de la tele/radio cuando te venga bien gastar la vida, pasar/perder mucho tiempo (en)
facilita permite hace posible hace (más) fácil hace (más) sencillo/a	la compra, la comunicación, el plagio, la banca electrónica, el robo de la identidad, la piratería, el acceso (a), la distribución rápida (de) ... la pornografía, el terrorismo, el acoso por Internet, información, un virus copiar, descargar, mandar, repartir ... (archivos, fotos, información, música)

WRITE

2 Put the following views into Spanish, using the grids.

1 The advantage of the Internet is that you can stay in touch with friends.

2 The good thing is that it's possible to get to know people from other countries and cultures.

3 The danger is that it makes identity theft easier.

4 The problem is that it makes access to pornography easier.

5 I like the Internet. You can keep up to date with what's happening.

6 It makes shopping possible for the housebound*.

7 You can watch TV programmes when it suits you.

8 The bad thing is that you can waste a lot of time on sites like Twitter.

*the housebound – las personas confinadas en su casa.

exam tip >>

The number of marks in brackets remind you how many pieces of information you need to give.

>> practice questions

SPEAK/WRITE

Prepare a paragraph answering the question: ¿Qué opinas tú de las nuevas tecnologías?

Listening section A

You will need to use the CD-ROM to complete this section.

A Personal details

>> **key fact** Revise the alphabet, months and numbers – they are often tested.

Rosa lives near the station. Listen and tick ✓ the correct box.

1 The name of the street is ...

| **a** Coinca ☐ | **b** Cuenca ☐ | **c** Cuince ☐ | **d** Toenca ☐ |

2 Her birthday is ...

| **a** 6/1 ☐ | **b** 26/2 ☐ | **c** 16/1 ☐ | **d** 16/2 ☐ |

B Descriptions

1 What did he look like? Write the appropriate letter in the box provided.

☐

2 What does Natalia always have with her? Answer in English in the space provided.

....

C Helping at home

>> **key fact** Learn expressions of frequency, like often (*muchas veces*), sometimes (*a veces, de vez en cuando*). They give you extra information which may be crucial.

1 ¿Qué hace Gema para ayudar en casa? Escribe ✓ en DOS casillas.

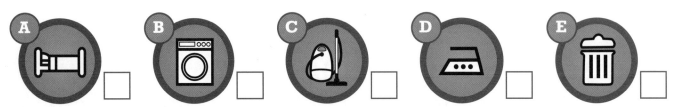

¿Qué opina de preparar la comida? Escribe ✓ en la casilla correcta.

A ☹ ☐   B ☺ ☐   C 😐 ☐   D zzzz ☹ ☐

D Daily routine

Make sure you are familiar with the 12- and 24-hour clock in Spanish.

Susanna talks about her daily routine. Fill the gaps in the sentences with the appropriate letters.

1   Susana gets up at ...

2   School begins at ...

3   She has lunch ...

4   She leaves school at ...

5   She does her homework ...

a 8.30	d 7.00	g 5.00
b at home	e in the library	h at a friend's house
c 4.00	f 7.30	i 8.00

E Relationships

>> **key fact** **In multiple-choice tasks, listen with care. The plural of a noun may have a different meaning to the singular, e.g. *hermano* – brother; *hermanos* – brothers or brothers and sisters...**

Lucía talks about her problem. Tick ✓ the correct answer.

1   **Lucía does not get on well with her ...**

a   best friend ☐

b   Dad ☐

c   parents ☐

2   **She is not allowed to ...**

a   stay out late ☐

b   go out with her friends ☐

c   have her party at the disco ☐

3   **She thinks it's**

a   not kind ☐

b   unfair ☐

c   boring ☐

4   **The problem is ...**

a   she's too young ☐

b   she's an only child ☐

c   she has to study ☐

Vocabulary

A My home

¿Vives en una casa o en un piso?	*Do you live in a house or a flat?*		
Vivo en (una casa) de (dos) plantas.	*I live in a (house) with (two) floors.*		
¿Cuántas habitaciones tiene?	*How many rooms has it got?*		
¿Cuáles son? Hay (una cocina ...)	*What are they? There's (a kitchen ...)*		
Descríbeme tu dormitorio: ¿cómo es?	*Describe your bedroom: what's it like?*		
Es grande/pequeño/mediano. Tiene ...	*It's big/small/medium-sized. It's got ...*		

una casa adosada	*a terraced house*	una cama	*a bed*
una chalet pareado	*a semi (-detached)*	una mesilla	*a bedside table*
un chalé, una finca	*a bungalow, a farm*	un guardarropa	*a wardrobe*
una torre	*a tower block*	un pupitre	*a desk*
una entrada	*a hall*	una silla/butaca	*a chair/armchair*
una puerta	*a door*	un tocador	*a dressing table*
un salón	*a living room*	un armario	*a cupboard*
un comedor	*a dining room*	una alfombra	*a rug*
las escaleras	*the stairs, staircase*	un estéreo	*a stereo*
(tres) dormitorios	*(three) bedrooms*	un televisor	*a TV set*
un cuarto de baño	*a bathroom*	un ordenador	*a computer*
da a	*looks out onto*	un jardín/césped	*garden/lawn*
una chimenea	*fireplace*	una estanteria	*bookcase*
las cortinas	*curtains*	la lámpara	*lamp*
el aseo	*toilet*	el radiador	*radiator*

B My town/village

¿Dónde vives? Vivo en (Newcastle).	*Where do you live? I live in Newcastle.*		
¿Dónde está exactamente?	*Where is it exactly?*		
Está en el (norte) de (Inglaterra).	*It's in the (north) of (England).*		
¿Cuál es tu dirección?	*What's your address?*		
La calle/avenida/plaza ..., número ...	*... street/avenue/square, number ...*		
Vivo en las afueras, en el centro	*I live in the outskirts, in the centre*		
en la sierra, en la costa, junto a un río	*in the mountains, on the coast, by a river*		
en una urbanización, en el barrio de ...	*on a housing estate, in the area of ...*		

hay ...	*there is/are ...*	un centro comercial	*a shopping centre*
colegios/institutos	*schools*	una pista de hielo	*an ice-rink*
bares, tiendas	*bars, shops*	una bolera	*a bowling alley*
restaurantes	*restaurants*	una piscina	*a pool*
un polideportivo	*a sports centre*	un teatro	*a theatre*
un cine	*a cinema*	una estación	*a station*

C Tourism

¿Cómo es el pueblo/la ciudad?		*What's the village/town like?*	
¿Qué hay en el barrio?		*What is there in the neighbourhood?*	
¿Qué se puede hacer? Se puede ...		*What can you do? You can ...*	
¿Dónde está la Oficina de Turismo?		*Where is the Tourist Office?*	
Estoy/estamos aquí de vacaciones.		*I am/we are here on holiday.*	
¿El restaurante está climatizado?		*Is the restaurant air-conditioned?*	

un mapa	*a map*	alquilar	*to hire*
un plano	*a town plan*	bañarse en el mar	*to bathe in the sea*
un folleto (sobre)	*a brochure (about)*	tomar el sol	*to sunbathe*
una guía turística	*a tourist guide (book)*	divertirse	*to enjoy oneself*
un horario (de)	*a timetable (of)*	pasarlo bien	*to have a good time*
una lista (de)	*a list (of)*	descansar	*to rest*
un albergue juvenil	*a youth hostel*	hacer turismo	*to sightsee*
una pensión	*bed and breakfast*	ir de excursión	*to take a trip*

D Weather

¿Qué tiempo hace?	*What's the weather like?*
Hace bueno, hace buen tiempo.	*The weather is good/fine.*
Hace malo, hace mal tiempo.	*The weather's bad.*
Hace/hará ... hay/habrá ...	*It is/it will be ... there is/there will be ...*

hace frío/calor	*it's cold/hot*	hay niebla/neblina	*there's fog/mist*
hace (mucho) sol	*it's (very) sunny*	hay hielo, granizo	*there's ice, hail*
hace viento	*it's windy*	hay tormenta	*there's a storm*
hay lluvia, llueve	*it's raining*	el cielo está ...	*the sky is ...*
hay nieve, nieva	*it's snowing*	despejado/nublado	*clear/cloudy*

E Travel and transport

Quisiera/quiero comprar/sacar ...	*I'd like to/I want to buy/get ...*
un billete de ida/un billete sencillo	*a single ticket*
un billete de ida y vuelta (para)	*a return ticket (to)*
un billete de primera/clase turista	*first/standard class ticket*
un compartimento (no) fumador	*a (non-) smoking compartment*
un bonobús	*a book of bus tickets*
¿A qué hora llega (el tren de ...)?	*When does (the train from ...) arrive?*
¿A qué hora sale (el autocar para ...)?	*When does (the coach for ...) leave?*
¿De qué andén sale?	*What platform does it leave from?*

Grammar

A Asking questions

English often uses 'do/does/don't' when asking questions.
You do not need it in Spanish – just put question marks round the sentence.

¿Quieres ir de excursión?	Do you want to go on a trip?
¿No quieres salir?	Don't you want to go out?

You can also use a question word:

¿dónde?	where?	¿cómo?	how?	¿quién(es)?	who?
¿adónde?	where to?	¿qué?	what?	¿de quién?	whose?
¿cuánto?	how much?	¿cuándo?	when?	¿por qué?	why?

¿Cuánto? is an adjective, so it agrees with the noun which follows it.

¡Cuánta gente en la playa!	What a lot of people on the beach!
¿Cuántos billetes quiere?	How many tickets do you want?
¿Cuántas personas vienen?	How many people are coming?

B A and De

A means 'to', and indicates 'away'. When followed by **el** it becomes **al**.

Voy a Madrid.	I'm going to Madrid.
¿A qué distancia está?	How far away is it?
Está a cien kilómetros.	It's a hundred kilometres away.
¿Vienes al bar?	Are you coming to the bar?

De means 'of'/'from'. When followed by **el** it becomes **del**.

Mi padre es de Granada.	My father is from Granada.
Un paquete de caramelos.	A packet of sweets.
Está delante del cine.	It's in front of the cinema.

Match up the halves of the sentences correctly. **Ejemplo: 1–c**

1	¿Por dónde se va al	a	… Madrid.
2	La cafetería está enfrente	b	… la panadería.
3	¿Felipe? Creo que es	c	… banco?
4	Perdone. ¿Para ir a los	d	… tiendas?
5	El estanco está detrás de	e	… farmacia, por favor?
6	Mañana, voy a ir a	f	… del mercado.
7	¿Por dónde se va a las	g	… de Murcia.
8	¿Cómo se va a la	h	… servicios?

C The immediate future

To indicate the immediate future – what is going to happen – use the verb **ir** *(to go)* followed by **a** and the infinitive of another verb:

yo	**voy**	*I go*	nosotros/as	**vamos**	*we go*
tú	**vas**	*you go*	vosotros/as	**vais**	*you go*
él	**va**	*he goes*	ellos	**van**	*they go*
ella	**va**	*she goes*	ellas	**van**	*they go*
usted	**va**	*you go*	ustedes	**van**	*you go*

Voy a estudiar francés.	*I'm going to study French.*
¿Qué vas a hacer en septiembre?	*What are you going to do in September?*
Vamos a salir a las ocho.	*We're going to leave at eight o'clock.*

D Positive commands

A positive command is an instruction to do something. Form them as follows:

-AR: **hablar** – *to speak*; -ER: **comer** – *to eat*; -IR: **escribir** – *to write*

TÚ	go to the **tú** form of the present tense and remove the final –s: habla(s) → habla, come(s) → come, escribe(s) → escribe
USTED	go to the **usted** form of the present tense and alter the last letter: habla → hable, come → coma, escribe → escriba

These verbs are irregular in some parts of their command form:

	cruzar (to cross)	torcer (to turn)	coger (to take)	seguir (to carry on)
TÚ	cruza	tuerce	coge	sigue
USTED	cruce	tuerza	coja	siga

E Relative pronouns

Relative pronouns link parts of a sentence together.

que who, that, which	La chica que vive allí. La casa, que es nueva ... *The girl who lives there. The house, that is new ...*
quién(es) who, whom	No sé quién vive allí. *I don't know who lives there.*
lo que what (that which)	No sé lo que quiere Marta. *I don't know what Marta wants.*

Complete each sentence with the correct relative pronoun.

a   Mi hermano, ... se llama Santi, tiene dieciocho años.

b   Creo que tiene novia, pero no sé .... es.

c   Santi dice que no le interesan las chicas, ¡ .... no es verdad!

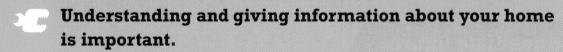

My home and bedroom

 Understanding and giving information about your home is important.

 You also need to be able to describe your bedroom in detail.

A My home

WRITE

Describe your home as fully as you can.

1 Let's look at how to improve your description of your home.

Read the information about Miguel's home below.

¿Cuántos adjetivos tiene? *How many adjectives does it have?*

remember >>

If the noun is feminine (una), then the adjectives which go with it must be feminine as well.

> Vivo en una casa[1] en las afueras de la ciudad. Tiene siete habitaciones: una entrada[2], una cocina[3], un salón comedor[4], un cuarto de baño y tres dormitorios. Hay una terraza[5] con flores. Delante de la casa[6] no hay jardín, pero al lado hay un garaje. Detrás hay un trozo de césped[7] y un patio[8] con una mesa y sillas.

It doesn't contain any adjectives at all! Let's improve it by adding some adjectives.

2 Use each of the adjectives 1–8 below after each of the nouns 1–8 in his letter.

Ejemplo: Vivo en una casa antigua …

1	antiguo/a (*old*)	**5**	espacioso/a (*spacious*)
2	pequeño/a (*small*)	**6**	bonito/a (*pretty*)
3	amueblado/a (*fitted*)	**7**	verde (*green*)
4	grande (*big*)	**8**	nuevo/a (*new*)

B Adding detail

READ

1 Miguel doesn't explain where things are. Include extra details for interest.

2 Match up the Spanish and English phrases below.

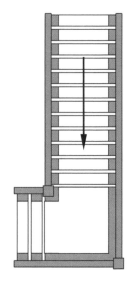

1	a la izquierda	**a**	*downstairs*
2	a la derecha	**b**	*which opens onto the terrace*
3	al fondo	**c**	*on the first floor*
4	en la planta baja	**d**	*upstairs*
5	en el primer piso	**e**	*on the left*
6	arriba	**f**	*altogether/in total*
7	abajo	**g**	*on the ground floor*
8	que da a la terraza	**h**	*at the end/back/rear*
9	en total	**i**	*on the right*

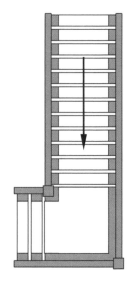

C My bedroom

Tres jóvenes hablan de sus dormitorios. Escribe el nombre correcto en la línea. *Three young people talk about their bedrooms. Write the correct name on the line.*

Gema

¡Mi dormitorio es el lugar más cómodo del mundo! Tiene armarios grandes, una cama doble, y una mesa enorme donde puedo hacer mis deberes o enviar emails a mis amigas. Todo está en su sitio. Las ventanas son grandes, pero la única cosa que no me gusta, es que desde el balcón se ve solamente la calle.

Pablo

Comparto mi dormitorio. La ventaja que tiene, es que es bastante grande – pero no es un lugar muy agradable. Primero, es como una cueva porque todas las paredes están pintadas de negro. Segundo, no hay mucha luz natural. Además, mi hermano deja su ropa sucia en el suelo. Nunca vale la pena arreglarlo.

Conchi

El problema es que mi cuarto es superpequeño. Hay sitio para una cama, una silla y nada más. Duermo allí, pero eso es todo. Para hacer mis deberes o jugar con el ordenador, tengo que ir al salón.

a El dormitorio no es grande. *Conchi*

b El dormitorio está en orden. ....

c No arregla su habitación. ....

d Es una habitación oscura. ....

e No pasa mucho tiempo en su dormitorio. ....

f Le gusta su dormitorio. ....

g Tiene un ordenador en su habitación. ....

h Tiene que compartir su cuarto. ....

i No tiene ordenador en su dormitorio. ....

j La vista desde la ventana no es muy bonita. ....

> **exam tip >>**
>
> **In the exam, read each sentence carefully. Remember that *no* (no) and *nunca/jamás* (never) change the meaning.**

>> practice questions

Write a detailed description of your home. Include the following details:

- the type of housing you live in
- how many rooms it has, and where they are
- where it is in the town/village
- which rooms are on which floor
- if it has a garden and garage
- include your opinion of it and mention its advantages, disadvantages or problems.

> **exam tip >>**
>
> **Use the phrases from C above: *la única cosa que no me gusta …* (the only thing I don't like …) *la ventaja que tiene, es que …* (it has the advantage that …), *el problema es que …* (the problem is that …).**

Local area

You need to understand information about a town or area, and describe your own.

Make sure you can explain what is good and bad about it.

A Places in the town

WRITE

Learn the Spanish for places in your town, so you can say or write them quickly and easily.

1 A **word map**, like the one below, is a good way of revising vocabulary.

2 Don't forget to write each with either **un** or **una**.

remember >>

After *no hay* you don't need *un* or *una*, e.g. *No hay discoteca.*

¿Qué hay en tu ciudad? Descríbela. *What is there in your town? Describe it.*

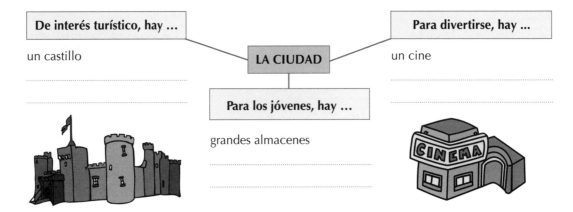

De interés turístico, hay ...		Para divertirse, hay ...
un castillo	**LA CIUDAD**	un cine
	Para los jóvenes, hay ...	
	grandes almacenes	

B Positives and negatives

SPEAK

exam tip >>

Describe your town fully to gain more marks.

Use the phrases below to describe your home town.

Describe tu ciudad: lo positivo y lo negativo.
Describe your town: the positive and the negative.

Lo malo/lo peor/el problema es que no hay ...
The bad thing/the worst thing/the problem is that there isn't a ... /aren't any ...

No hay nada que hacer. No hay nada para (los jóvenes). ¡Está muerta!
There's nothing to do. There's nothing for (young people). It's dead!

Hay mucha contaminación/pobreza. Hay mucho desempleo.
There's a lot of pollution/poverty. There's a lot of unemployment.

Lo bueno/lo mejor/lo que me gusta es que hay ...
The good thing/the best thing/what I like is that there is a .../there are ...

Hay mucho que hacer. Hay muchas distracciones.
There's lots to do. There's lots of entertainment.

Hay mucho comercio/turismo/verde/dinero en la zona.
There's a lot of business activity/tourism/green land/ wealth in the area.

C Understanding descriptions

READ

1 In the exam, you may be asked to read a description, along with a list of items which can be in English or Spanish. Your task is to decide which of the items are mentioned in the description.

2 Read through the list of items first, so you know what you are looking for.

3 Think of several Spanish words you might see for each item:

Ejemplo: either **moderno** (modern) and **nuevo** (new) could describe the 'new part' of a town.

remember >>

Negatives make a difference to the meaning! Learn these: *no … nunca/ jamás* (never), *no … nada* (nothing), *no … nadie* (no-one).

Lee el correo electrónico de Santi. ¿De qué habla? Escribe las cinco letras correctas.
Read Santi's email. What does he talk about? Write down the five correct letters.

a the old part of the town

b schools

c entertainment

d the new part of the town

e banks

f the countryside

g travel zones

h shopping facilities

i campsites

j problems with finding work

¡Hola! Me llamo Santi y vivo en el norte de Colombia. Mi ciudad se llama Cartagena. De interés turístico, hay una parte antigua y monumentos como la catedral y el Palacio de la Inquisición. Para ir de compras, hay tiendas turísticas y un mercado. Para divertirse, hay playa, una fiesta local (en marzo), muchos clubs y discotecas, y un cine. Pero si te gustan las distracciones, hay que tener dinero – ¡y nadie lo tiene! ¿Cómo es mi ciudad? Es histórica y bonita, pero también ruidosa y un poco sucia. ¿Y la región? Por un lado hay mucho turismo y mucho comercio; por otro, en algunas zonas hay mucho desempleo. Lo bueno es que está situada en un entorno rural muy bonito, pero el problema es que no hay mucho para los jóvenes en los pueblos.

>> practice questions

You are preparing a web page about your own town/area for Santi's school. List in Spanish, in bullet point form, the good things and the bad things about it. Use the phrases in Activity B and adapt sentences from Santi's email.

exam tip >>

You can make brief notes/bullet points in Spanish in preparation for the writing assessment. Check how many words you are allowed – make every one count!

Tourist information

A In the Tourist Office

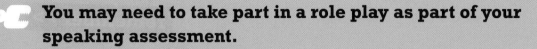 >> **key fact** You will have to cope with an element of unpredictability in a role-play. Make sure that you can answer personal questions and say how long you have been learning Spanish.

WRITE

Anita (**A**) has a part-time job in her local Tourist Office. A Spanish visitor (**V**) arrives. Read the conversation and choose the correct sentence for each gap from the answers on the facing page.

V	1	....
A	¡Claro que sí! Hablo español – lo estudio en el instituto.	
V	2	....
A	Es gratis. Aquí tiene – al dorso hay una lista de servicios también.	
V	3	....
A	Hay un castillo, que data del siglo trece, las murallas antiguas, y en el puerto se puede ver la casa más pequeña de Gran Bretaña.	
V	4	....
A	Está abierto ahora, y hoy cierra a las cinco.	
V	5	....
A	¿Cuántos años tienen?	
V	6	....
A	El parque de mariposas es muy interesante, y hay excursiones en barco por la costa.	
V	7	....
A	Salen del puerto, allí abajo. Hay excusiones cada hora y duran unos cuarenta minutos.	
V	8	....
A	Lo siento, no quedan. Pero hay una guía electronica allí en el rincón, que tiene todos los detalles de la red de transporte en la zona.	
V	9	....
A	Desde hace tres años. Me encanta practicar porque tengo exámenes pronto, pero ¡entiendo más que hablo!	
V	10	....

a ¿De dónde salen los barcos?

b Mireia tiene once y Pepe catorce.

c ¿Tiene un horario de trenes?

d ¡Qué interesante! ¿A qué hora abre el castillo?

e ¡Eso es normal! Y su español es mejor que mi inglés. Muchísimas gracias ¡y buena suerte! Adiós...

f ¡Qué bien! Primero, ¿tiene un plano de la ciudad? ¿Cuánto cuesta?

g Y para los niños, ¿qué hay en cuanto a diversiones?

h Vale, muchas gracias. Usted habla muy bien – ¿cuánto tiempo hace que estudia español?

i Buenos días. Estamos aquí de vacaciones, pero no hablamos inglés. ¿Nos puede ayudar?

j ¿Y qué hay de interés turístico en la ciudad?

For one of the speaking assessments, you may have to play a role, asking for or giving information. Using the conversation above as a model, work out how to talk about the following facilities in Spanish.

>> practice questions

Cathedral
(Fourteenth Century)

Open daily 08.00–18.00, (Free)

Like messing about in boats?

Try *River Trips!*

Modern boat, sailings every two hours, snacks and drinks included.

**Depart opposite bus station.
Reductions for families!**

Old Market
(18th century), **every morning 08.00–13.00**

Regional foods, organic produce, crafts and gifts.

Sports Centre and Swimming Pool
daily 10.00–20.00

Volleyball, squash, table tennis, classes in summer.

Railway Museum

Open Sat/Sun
10.00–17.00
£2.00 adults, £1.00 children
(Under 5s free)

Skateway Ice Rink
Tues–Sun,
12 noon till 9.00 p.m.
Closed Mondays

Weather and climate

You need to be able to get the gist of weather forecasts.

You will have to understand information about climate in areas of Spain.

A Talking about the weather

SPEAK

Make sure you know the basic weather expressions.

1 You may be asked about the climate in your area in the conversation part of the exam, or have to describe the weather in a role-play.

2 Practise, using the symbols below.

3 Say what the weather is like in each area.

En el norte ...

En las montañas ...

En el sur ... **25**

En la costa ... **-4**

4 You may also hear **el litoral** (coast) and **la meseta** (plateau, high flat area).

B Forecasts

Learn families of words to do with weather.

1 Within groups or families of words describing weather, there are similarities and clues which can help you understand forecasts.

2 Without using a dictionary, can you put each phrase a–n into its correct 'family'?

Ejemplo:

lluvia (rain)	calor (heat)	nubes (clouds)	frío (cold)
b		d	

a bajas temperaturas

b día lluvioso

c hielo en las carreteras

d cielo nublado

e temperaturas llegarán hasta los 30 grados

f llueve mucho en el norte

g vientos calientes del sur

h lloverá mañana

i aumento de nubosidad

j temperaturas altas en la costa

k caluroso/a

l húmedo/a

m temperaturas suaves

n nevar

The autonomous communities

READ

It is important to know about different areas in Spain for the exam.

How good is your knowledge of the autonomous communities of Spain? Choose the correct area of Spain (a–s) for each number on the map.

a Andalucía
b Aragón
c Cantabria
d Cataluña
e Asturias
f Extremadura
g La Rioja
h Melilla
i Murcia
j Navarra
k Ceuta
l Galicia
m Castilla y León
n Castilla La Mancha
o País Vasco (Euskadi)
p Comunidad de Madrid
q Comunidad Valenciana
r Baleares
s Canarias

Comunidades Autónomas de España

practice questions

Read about Spain's climate. Write the correct word in each space.

El clima de España es muy variado. En el norte y noroeste, las comunidades de Galicia, Cantabria, País Vasco, Navarra y Aragón tienen veranos suaves y húmedos, con inviernos lluviosos bajo la influencia del mar Cantábrico. En el centro, sobre todo en la meseta, el clima es continental – es decir, nieve y bajas temperaturas en invierno y seco en verano. El litoral este y sur tiene un clima mediterráneo, con veranos bastante calurosos y secos, y los inviernos más fríos y húmedos. En el sur se encuentra la España seca, en las comunidades de Murcia y Andalucía: temperaturas muy altas en verano, suaves en invierno, y muy poca lluvia en cualquier estación del año.

1 **The northern coastal areas have _____ and _____ summers.**

2 **In the central plateau, winters are _____ and summers are _____**

3 **Mediterranean areas enjoy _____ temperatures in summer.**

4 **Murcia has _____ summers and _____ rainfall.**

a mild
b snowy
c damp
d dry
e low
f high
g very hot
f high
h very little
i very wet

Vocabulary

A Asking the way

¿Hay (un bar/una farmacia) por aquí?	*Is there (a bar/a chemist's) near here?*
Sí, hay (uno/una) en ... Está/están ...	*Yes, there's (one) in ... It is/they are ...*
delante (de), detrás (de), enfrente (de), lejos (de)	*in front (of), behind, opposite, far (from)*
al lado (de), debajo (de), cerca (de),	*beside, underneath/below, near (to),*
¿Por dónde se va a ...? ¿Para ir a ...?	*How do you get to ...?*
Tome/coja, tuerza, cruce	*Take, turn, cross*
la primera/segunda/tercera (calle)	*the first/second/third (street)*
a la izquierda, a la derecha, entre	*on the left, on the right, between*
Siga todo recto (hasta ...)	*Carry straight on (as far as ...)*

B Environment

¿Qué debemos hacer ...	*What should we do ...*
para proteger el medio ambiente?	*to protect the environment?*
(No) debemos/deberíamos (utilizar) ...	*We must/should (not) (use) ...*
vidrio, papel, bolsas de plástico, agua	*glass, paper, plastic bags, water*
Debe haber más/menos ...	*There ought to be more/less, fewer ...*
Me preocupa .../me molesta ...	*I'm worried about .../I get upset about ...*
la contaminación/la polución, la ecología	*pollution, ecology*

sería mejor ...	*it would be better ...*	estropear	*to spoil, damage*
reducir, reciclar	*to reduce, to recycle*	contaminar	*to contaminate*
utilizar, reutilizar	*to use, to reuse*	matar, quemar	*to kill, to burn*
ahorrar, malgastar	*to save, to waste*	podría ser .../es ...	*it could be .../it is ...*
consumir, salvar	*to consume, to save*	dañino/a, ecológico	*harmful, ecological*
producir, evitar	*to produce, to avoid*	desastroso/a	*disastrous*
arruinar, amenazar	*to ruin, to threaten*	imprudente	*reckless*
controlar, destruir	*to control, to destroy*	peligroso/a	*dangerous*

el aire, el mar	*air, sea*	la marea negra	*oil slick*
el atasco	*traffic jam*	la naturaleza	*nature*
la basura	*rubbish*	el planeta, la sequía	*planet, drought*
la circulación	*traffic*	el recurso natural	*natural resource*
el desastre	*disaster*	el reciclaje	*recycling*
la destrucción	*destruction*	la selva, la tierra	*jungle, earth*
la energía	*energy*	el tráfico, el vehículo	*traffic, vehicle*
la extinción	*extinction*	la urbanización	*housing estate*
la gasolina (sin plomo)	*(unleaded) petrol*	la vivienda	*housing, house*
el gasóleo	*diesel (oil)*	la capa de ozono	*ozone layer*
la inundación	*flood*	el contenedor	*recycling bin*

Grammar

C · Negative commands

To instruct someone NOT to do something, take the **yo** form of the present tense, remove the final **-o**, and add these endings:

		TÚ	VOSOTROS/AS	USTED	USTEDES
-ar	hablo	no hables	no habléis	no hable	no hablen
-er	como	no comas	no comáis	no coma	no coman
-ir	escribo	no escribas	no escribáis	no escriba	no escriban

This holds true if the **yo** form is irregular: e.g. **salir** (**yo salgo**), **poner** (**yo pongo**).

Señor, no hable tan rápido.	*Sir, do not talk so fast.*
¡No comáis chicle!	*Don't eat chewing-gum!*
¡No salgas, Marta, por favor!	*Don't go out, Marta, please!*
¡No ponga el libro allí!	*Don't put the book there!*

D · Impersonal verbs

These are verbs which follow the same pattern as **gustar**. You will need an indirect object pronoun: **me**, **te**, **le**, **nos**, **os**, **les** (p. 13).

doler (*to hurt*)	Me duele la cabeza. (*My head hurts me.*)
encantar (*to delight*)	Le encanta el fútbol. (*Football delights him.*)
faltar (*to be lacking*)	Me falta un tenedor. (*A fork is lacking to me.*)
hacer falta (*to be necessary*)	Me hace falta más tiempo. (*More time is necessary to me.*)
interesar (*to interest*)	Me interesa mucho el golf. (*Golf interests me.*)
quedar (*to remain*)	Me quedan dos galletas. (*Two biscuits are left to me.*)
sobrar (*to be left over*)	Le sobra pan. (*Bread is left over to him.*)

The literal meanings are given in brackets. Can you put them into better English?

E · Adverbs

Adverbs describe verbs and actions. They are words like 'quickly', 'suddenly'.

Take the feminine form of the adjective, and add -**mente**:

ADJECTIVE	FEMININE FORM	ADD -MENTE	
entusiasmado	entusiasmada	entusiasmadamente	*enthusiastically*
triste	triste	tristemente	*sadly*

Some common adverbs have other forms:

bien (*well*), **mal** (*badly*), **despacio** (*slowly*), **rápido/rápidamente** (*quickly*).

When there are two adverbs together, the first one loses the **-mente**:

Conduce cuidadosa y lentamente. *He drives carefully and slowly.*

Finding the way

 Exchange information about location and facilities.

 You need to understand and give directions.

A Asking where a place is

>> **key fact** Expressions of courtesy are useful in many contexts.

SPEAK

 Stop a passer-by: **Perdone, señor/señora/señorita.**

Be polite: **¿Me puede decir si ...?** *(Can you tell me if ...?)*

End courteously: **Muchas gracias** *(Many thanks)*. **De nada** *(Don't mention it)*.

Usa el mapa para contestar a las preguntas. *Use the map to answer the questions.*

Ejemplo: ¿Hay un banco por aquí? – Sí, hay uno en la calle Goya.

1 ¿Hay un estanco por aquí?

2 ¿Hay una cafetería por aquí?

3 ¿Hay una farmacia cerca?

4 ¿Hay servicios por aquí?

5 No veo el mercado. ¿Hay uno?

6 ¿Hay una parada de autobús por aquí?

7 ¿Hay tiendas de recuerdos en esta parte de la ciudad?

Revise prepositions of place ('behind', 'next to', etc.) on page 36.

Work out what you need to put in the gaps below, using the map.

Turista: Perdone, señora. ¿Hay un estanco ...(1)... aquí?

Señora: Sí, hay ...(2)... en la avenida de Cádiz.

Turista: ¿Dónde está exactamente?

Señora: Está ...(3)... del mercado, y ...(4)... la cafetería y las tiendas de recuerdo.

Turista: Muchas ...(5)... .

Señora: De ...(6)..., adiós.

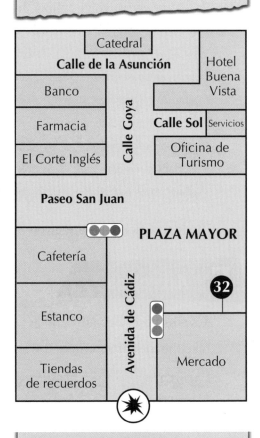

remember >>

In questions, use *hay* followed by *un* or *una* except for *correos*. In the reply, *un* becomes *uno/una*: *Hay uno en la plaza.* (There is one in the square.)

remember >>

When *de* is followed by *el*, it becomes *del*.

B Directions

READ

1 Check first that you know your directions!

2 Unscramble the following phrases 1–10. Write the English for each one.

1 la baje calle
2 izquierda a tuerza la
3 izquierda a primera la tome la
4 recto todo siga
5 calle de final al la

6 plaza cruce la
7 a tuerza derecha la
8 la a la tome derecha segunda
9 el siga cruce hasta
10 semáforos los hasta

remember >>

Learn useful words like *primero* (first), *luego* (then), *después* (afterwards), *finalmente* (finally), *izquierda* (left), *derecha* (right).

3 You may have to read a series of directions, and decide where they take you. Use the map on page 38. Begin at the bottom at ✳.

Lee las instrucciones: ¿adónde llegas? Escribe el nombre del lugar. *Read the directions. Where do you get to? Write the name of the place.*

1 Siga todo recto. Está al final de la calle Goya, enfrente.

2 Siga hasta el semáforo enfrente del estanco, y luego tuerza a la derecha. Está allí, delante de la parada de autobús número treinta y dos.

3 Siga todo recto, hasta el cruce. En el semáforo, tuerza a la izquierda. Hay una entrada enfrente de la cafetería.

4 Hay que seguir todo recto, hasta el cruce con el paseo San Juan, y luego sigue un poco más lejos. Coge la calle a la derecha, y están allí mismo, enfrente.

5 Está a unos cinco minutos andando. Siga todo recto, y coja la calle Goya. Al final, tuerza a la izquierda. La entrada está allí, a mano izquierda.

>> practice questions

Answer the questions in Spanish using the map on page 38.

1 Perdone, ¿por dónde se va al Corte Inglés?

2 ¿Para ir al Hotel Buena Vista, por favor?

3 ¿Me puede decir si hay una farmacia por aquí? ¿Cómo se va?

4 ¿Por dónde se va a la cafetería, por favor?

exam tip >>

If you realise you've made a mistake in the role-play part of the exam, say *Lo siento, me he equivocado*, and then try again.

Travel and transport

A In the street

 READ

Learn names of shops and places in the town.

You need to understand simple signs and notices in the street and in shops.

The task below asks you to match up each sign with the appropriate shop. This kind of task often has one or more possibilities left over. Try the ones you know first. Be careful – there are two which mention 'estudiante'!

Escribe la letra correcta en cada casilla. *Write the correct letter in each box.*

1 ☐
2 ☐
3 ☐
4 ☐
5 ☐
6 ☐
7 ☐
8 ☐

a   la zapatería
b   la estación de RENFE
c   la tabaquería/el estanco
d   el colegio
e   el quiosco
f   la pastelería
g   la estación de autobuses
h   los grandes almacenes
i   la frutería

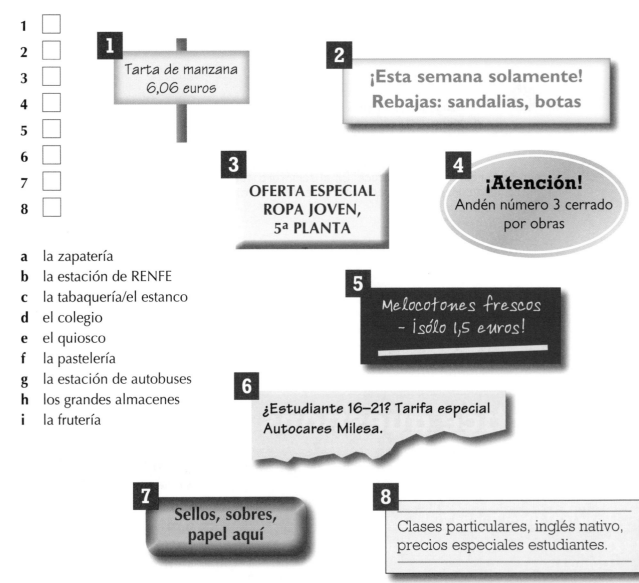

1
Tarta de manzana
6,06 euros

2
¡Esta semana solamente!
Rebajas: sandalias, botas

3
OFERTA ESPECIAL
ROPA JOVEN,
5ª PLANTA

4
¡Atención!
Andén número 3 cerrado
por obras

5
Melocotones frescos
– ¡sólo 1,5 euros!

6
¿Estudiante 16–21? Tarifa especial
Autocares Milesa.

7
Sellos, sobres,
papel aquí

8
Clases particulares, inglés nativo,
precios especiales estudiantes.

B Means of travel

READ

1. First, study the pictures carefully – what do they show?

2. What word(s) do(es) each one suggest to you?

   Escribe la letra correcta en cada casilla. *Write the correct letter in each box.*

   1 Semana de la Salud, mayo 7–14: ¡Venid al instituto a pie! ☐

   2 ¿Te interesa visitar Gran Bretaña? Octubre 15-22, viaje en avión. ☐

   3 Autocar Centro-Río Rosas. Salida 14.40. ☐

   4 ¡Perdido! Permiso de tren. Ana Vallejas 1° de la ESO ☐

   5 ¡Si vas en moto, hay que llevar casco! ☐

   6 Nuevo – soporte para bicicletas, detrás del gimnasio. ☐

C Getting around

WRITE

1. You may need to give your opinion on travel in your area:

   a getting to and from places   **b** how long it takes   **c** pros and cons of different types of transport

2. Read the conversation and choose the correct words in brackets for Pepita. She lives quite far away from school, travels by train (quick and comfortable, but expensive), and it takes about twenty minutes.

   + ¿Cómo vienes al instituto cada día?

   − Vengo *(en autobús, en tren, en bicicleta, en coche, en metro, andando)*.

   + ¿Por qué?

   − Vivo *(bastante, muy) (cerca, lejos)* del instituto.

   + ¿Te gusta?

   − Es *(rápido, lento, cómodo, incómodo, barato, caro, divertido, aburrido, ruidoso, tranquilo)*.

   + ¿Cuánto tiempo tardas en llegar?

   − Tardo *(unos ... minutos, media hora, alrededor de una hora)*.

   + ¿Qué problemas tienes en ir por ahí?

   − *(El problema (la (des)ventaja)* es que los gastos de viajar en transporte público son *(grandes/enormes/demasiados/bajos/altos)* para la gente joven.

>> practice questions

Prepare your own replies to the questions above, using the phrases given. Practise with a friend.

study hint >>

Give details of each form of transport you use and the order in which you use them.

The environment

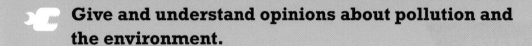

- Give and understand opinions about pollution and the environment.

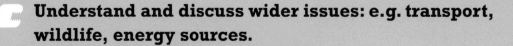

- Understand and discuss wider issues: e.g. transport, wildlife, energy sources.

A Improving the environment

WRITE

This is a good topic in which to use the conditional tense.

1 You need to be able to talk and write about the environment.

What do you think we should do, or shouldn't do:

a **within the home** environment?

b **in the street** – in what we buy, use or throw away?

c **in general**, to protect our environment?

2 Give us your view: what is the English for each of the following?

a en mi opinión

b Personalmente

c yo creo que

d a mi modo de ver

e desde mi punto de vista

3 Use the grids below to help you work out what you want to say.

Escribe tres frases para expresar tu opinión con la ayuda de los recuadros. *Write three sentences to express your opinion. Use the grids to help you.*

Ejemplo: En el hogar, deberíamos ahorrar más agua, y no debemos utilizar tantos envases de plástico.

A En el hogar ...
In the home

B En la calle ...
In the street

C En general ...
In general

(No)	debemos	utilizar, reutilizar, reciclar, ahorrar
	deberíamos	gastar, tirar, echar, comprar, consumir
	sería mejor	producir, reducir la cantidad de ...
más/menos	tanto	vidrio, papel, plástico, gasóleo
	tanta	agua, ropa, gasolina, basura
	tantos	contenedores, recursos naturales
	tantas	bolsas (de plástico)

remember >>

Tanto (as/so much, as/so many) is an adjective. It must be the same gender (masculine, feminine) and number (singular, plural) as the noun it describes: *tanto vidrio* (as/so much glass), *tantas bolsas* (as/so many bags).

42

B Transport issues

>> key fact **You will not usually be expected to write more than a few words.**

READ

1 In the reading exam, you may have to write answers in Spanish.

2 There may be a word, or words, in the text which you can reuse in your answer.

3 You may need to use the verb form of a noun given in the text, or vice-versa.

4 Use the following hints to help:

Leonora: After **de**, you will need a noun or a verb.

Adriano: After **es**, you will need an adjective here.

Paco: After **se puede**, you will need a verb.

Completa las frases en español. *Complete the sentences in Spanish.*

> **remember >>**
>
> **There may be words you don't know in the reading texts. Unfamiliar but important words will have an English explanation.**

En el centro nuevo de mi ciudad hay calles anchas para los coches, y se puede circular fácilmente. Sin embargo hay mucho tráfico en los barrios más antiguos, donde suele haber atascos.

Leonora

En mi ciudad necesitamos una red* de transporte público más eficiente, pero también más barata. Muchos jóvenes no tienen bastante dinero para pagar los billetes.

Adriano

* red = *network*

Ahora que tengo mi carné de conducir, puedo ir al centro comercial nuevo sin problemas. Hay muchos aparcamientos, y además son gratis.

Paco

Leonora: En el centro, no hay problemas de ....

Adriano: El problema para los jóvenes es que el transporte es ....

Paco: Lo bueno es que se puede .... fácilmente.

>> practice questions

How might you answer the following questions in the speaking part of the exam?

¿Cómo se puede proteger el medio ambiente?
(How can we protect the environment?)

¿Cómo se puede mejorar tu ciudad?
(How could your town be improved?)

En tu/su opinión, ¿cuáles son los problemas más importantes del medio ambiente?
(In your opinion, which are the most important issues as regards the environment?)

> **exam tip >>**
>
> **As well as your opinion, you can add expressions which indicate your feelings:** *me molesta/n ...* **(... bothers me),** *me preocupa/n por ...* **(worries me ...).**

Listening section B

You will need to use the CD-ROM to complete this section.

A My home

>> **key fact** Read the sentences carefully before listening. Sometimes a word (e.g. supermarket) appears in two places.

1 How does Marta describe her house?
Write the correct letter in the box.

A	detached, next to supermarket
B	terraced house, near school
C	flat near supermarket

2 What does she think of her home?
Write the correct letter in the box.

A	quite old and comfortable
B	old and ugly
C	comfortable and pretty

3 What's the best thing about her house?
Write the correct letter in the box.

A	far away from school
B	she gets there nice and early
C	doesn't have to get up early

B My town

1 What can you do in the town?
Write the correct letters in the boxes.

2 What is there to do in Miguel's home town?
Put a tick ✔ in the correct boxes.

C Opinions

>> **key fact** Listen carefully for expressions which suggest a point of view: e.g. *lo bueno/lo malo*, especially if you hear them in the same extract.

What do these young people think about the area they live in?
Beside each name write:

P (Positive)
N (Negative)
P + N (Positive and Negative)

Andrés   Julia   Karim

D Weather and climate

1 Íñigo talks about his thoughts for the future. Complete the gaps in English.

a Íñigo would like to live .... in Spain.

b He prefers ....

and he likes to ....

2 Íñigo talks about the weather. Tick three boxes for each season.

>> **key fact** Listen very carefully. You might think that 'hot' and 'sunny'
go together, but that is not necessarily true.

Winter	rain	snow	cold	wind	ice

Summer	hot	sunny	pleasant	mild	not too hot

E Transport

At the train station.
Put a tick beside the three (3) correct answers.

1	type of ticket	return	
2	class of ticket	second	
3	platform number	7	
4	cost in euros	5 euros 36	
5	train usually leaves at	10.00	
6	but problem today	5 minute delay	

exam tip >>

**Revise the numbers
1–50 before listening!**

F Environment

>> **key fact** Learn words which indicate quite (*bastante*) very (*muy*), too much
(*demasiado*) etc. They can make all the difference to the answer.

Which problems worry Santi most? Complete the sentences in English with one word.

a There are too many ....

b There are many people who don't ....

c It's a .... thing we could all do.

Vocabulary

A Shopping

¿Dónde puedo comprar ...? Busco ...	Where can I buy ... ? I'm looking for ...
¿Tiene ... ? ¿Hay ... ? ¿Se vende ... ?	Do you have ... ? Are there ... ? Do you sell ... ?
Quisiera ... . ¿Me pone/da ... por favor?	I'd like ... . Can you give me ... please?
¿Es eso todo? Sí, eso es todo.	Is that everything? Yes, that's the lot.
¿Algo más? No, nada más, gracias.	Anything else? No, nothing else, thanks.
¿Tiene cambio? No tengo cambio.	Have you got any change? I don't have change.
Sólo tengo un billete de (50) euros.	I've only got a (50) euro note.
¿Se puede pagar con cheque?	Can you pay by cheque?
con tarjeta de crédito, en metálico/efectivo	by credit card, in cash

una carnicería	a butcher's	una panadería	a baker's
una confitería	a sweet shop	una pastelería	a cake shop
una droguería	toiletries shop/chemist's	una pescadería	a fishmonger's
un estanco	a tobacconist's	una peluquería	a hairdresser's
una frutería	a greengrocer's	un quiosco	a kiosk, stall
los grandes almacenes	department store	un supermercado	a supermarket
el hipermercado	hypermarket	una tienda de comestibles	food store
una joyería	jeweller's	una tienda de ropa	a clothes shop
una juguetería	toy shop	una tabaquería	a tobacconist's
una librería	book shop	una zapatería	a shoe shop

un abrigo	a coat	un pantalón	a pair of trousers
un bañador	a swimming costume	un pantalón corto	a pair of shorts
una blusa/camisa	a blouse/shirt	la ropa	clothes
una camiseta	a T-shirt	un sombrero, una gorra	a hat, a cap
un chandal	a track suit	las medias/los calcetines	stockings/socks
una chaqueta	jacket	los guantes	gloves
un cinturón	a belt	los vaqueros	jeans
una corbata	a tie	el vestido	dress
una falda, un jersey	a skirt, a jersey	las sandalias	sandals
un impermeable	a raincoat	zapatos, zapatillas	shoes, slippers
la moda	fashion	zapatillas de deporte	trainers

a mitad de precio	half price	una oferta	(special) offer
un bolso, una caja	bag, till/box	un paraguas	umbrella
un collar	necklace	los pendientes	earrings
un disco compacto	a CD	un precio, un recibo	price, receipt
elegir, escoger	to choose	un regalo, un juguete	present, toy
las gafas de sol	sunglasses	un reloj	watch, clock
gastar, pagar	to spend, to pay	el (teléfono) móvil	mobile (phone)

¿Qué ponen en la tele/el cine?	*What's on TV/at the cinema?*
Ponen una película de acción/de terror.	*There's an action/horror film on.*
una película de ciencia-ficción, una comedia	*A science-fiction film, a comedy*
una película de aventuras, una telenovela	*An adventure film, a soap opera.*
una película romántica/policíaca, un concierto	*A romantic/detective film, a concert*
¿Cuánto cuestan las entradas?	*How much are the tickets?*
¿Dónde están los asientos? Arriba/abajo.	*Where are the seats? Upstairs/downstairs.*
¿A qué hora empieza/termina (la sesión)?	*What time does the (showing) start/finish?*

una aficionado/a	*a fan*	Gran Hermano	*Big Brother*
los anuncios, actuar	*adverts, perform*	el/la jugador/a, el ocio	*player, leisure*
el ambiente, un/a artista	*atmosphere, artist*	la pantalla	*screen*
un baile	*a dance*	un partido	*a match*
un/a campeón/ona	*a champion*	un pasatiempo	*pastime*
un campeonato	*a championship*	el premio, una pelota	*prize, ball*
una carrera	*race*	la publicidad	*the advertising*
una cartelera	*an entertainment guide*	las noticias	*the news*
el comienzo	*start, beginning*	una revista	*magazine*
un concurso	*a quiz-show, contest*	una sala de fiestas	*hall*
una copa	*cup, trophy*	una salida, una sesión	*outing/exit, showing*
una corrida	*a bull-fight*	un/a socio/a	*member*
dibujos animados	*cartoons*	el sonido	*sound*
un documental	*a documentary*	el telediario	*the news*
educativo/a	*educative*	la taquilla	*the box-office*
un espectáculo, un equipo	*show, team*	el tebeo, los toros	*comic, the bulls*
un estadio, una estrella	*stadium, star*	el videoclub	*videoclub*
una función	*a show*	el videojuego	*videogame*

C Restaurants

¿Qué quiere tomar (de primero/segundo)?	*What would you like for the first/second course?*
de postre, para beber	*for dessert, to drink*
Quisiera, para mí, para mi (amigo/a)	*I'd like, I'll have, my (friend) will have*
¿Qué hay para vegetarianos?	*What is there for vegetarians?*
¿Qué es ... exactamente? ¿Contiene ... ?	*What is ... exactly? Does it contain ... ?*
¿El servicio está incluido? ¿(El pan) es gratis?	*Is the service included? Is (the bread) free?*
¿Me cobra, por favor? Falta un/una ...	*Can I pay, please? We're missing a ...*
El vaso/la cuchara está sucio/a.	*The glass/ the spoon is dirty.*
un cuchillo, un tenedor	*a knife, a fork*

Grammar

A The preterite tense

The preterite tense explains what happened.
For example: *I went to Spain; I visited the capital; I ate out at night.*

The following are regular

	-ar (hablar)	-er (comer)	-ir (vivir)
yo	habl**é**	com**í**	viv**í**
tú	habl**aste**	com**iste**	viv**iste**
él, ella, usted	habl**ó**	com**ió**	viv**ió**
nosotros/as	habl**amos**	com**imos**	viv**imos**
vosotros/as	habl**asteis**	com**isteis**	viv**isteis**
ellos, ellas, ustedes	habl**aron**	com**ieron**	viv**ieron**

The following are irregular. Note that **ser** *(to be)* and **ir** *(to go)* are the same

SER *(to be)*	fui, fuiste, fue, fuimos, fuisteis, fueron
IR *(to go)*	fui, fuiste, fue, fuimos, fuisteis, fueron
DAR *(to give)*	di, diste, dio, dimos, disteis, dieron

B The pretérito grave

The following verbs have a change to their stem, and different endings.
(The stem is the part which is left when you remove the **-ar**, **-er**, **-ir**).

INFINITIVE		STEM	INFINITIVE		STEM
to walk	andar	anduv-	*to put, lay, set*	poner	pus-
to say	decir	dij-	*to want*	querer	quis-
to be	estar	estuv-	*to know*	saber	sup-
to do, make	hacer	hic-/hiz	*to have*	tener	tuv-
to be able to	poder	pud-	*to come*	venir	vin-

Add these endings to the stems above:

yo	-e	nosotros/as	-imos
tú	-iste	vosotros/as	-isteis
él, ella, usted	-o	ellos, ellas, ustedes	-ieron

Estuve en el centro todo el día.	*I was in the centre all day.*
Hicimos mucho turismo.	*We did a lot of sightseeing.*

C Time phrases

ayer, anteayer, anoche	*yesterday, the day before yesterday, last night*
hace dos días, el año pasado, la semana pasada	*two days ago, last year, last week*

D Direct object pronouns

Direct object pronouns in English are: *me, you, him, her, it, us, them*. In Spanish they are:

SINGULAR		PLURAL	
me (*m/f*)	*me*	nos (*m/f*)	*us*
te (*m/f*)	*you (informal)*	os (*m/f*)	*you (informal)*
lo (*m*)	*it, him, you (formal)*	los (*m*)	*them, you (formal)*
la (*f*)	*it, her, you (formal)*	las (*f*)	*them, you (formal)*
le* (*m*)	*him, you (formal)*		

*In some areas of Spain and South America, you may hear **le** also used for *her*, and **les** for *them* when referring to people (*both masculine and feminine*).

¿Qué? No te oigo bien.	*What? I can't hear you clearly.*
¿El bañador? Sí, lo compro.	*The swimming costume? Yes, I'm buying it.*
La falda ... . No la quiero.	*The skirt ... . I don't want it.*
¿Los calcetines? Sí, me los llevo.	*The socks? Yes, I'll take them.*
¿Juan? No lo/le veo.	*Juan? I don't see him.*

E Demonstrative adjectives and pronouns

1 Use demonstrative adjectives for *this ..., that ..., those ...*:

	(*ms*)	(*fs*)		(*mpl*)	(*fpl*)
this	este	esta	*these*	estos	estas
that	ese	esa	*those*	esos	esas
that (over there)	aquel	aquella	*those (over there)*	aquellos	aquellas

No me gusta esta chaqueta.	*I don't like this jacket.*
Ese chandal es caro.	*That tracksuit is expensive.*
Aquel cinturón es más barato.	*That belt over there is cheaper.*
Aquellos vaqueros son bonitos.	*Those jeans over there are nice.*

Demonstrative pronouns (*this one, that one, those ones*) are the same as the demonstrative adjectives above. You may see them with an accent, but this is no longer necessary.

¿Un abrigo? – ¿Te gusta éste/este?	*A coat? – Do you like this one?*
Quiero una camiseta. – ¿Cuánto es ésa/esa?	*I want a T-shirt. – How much is that one?*

2 Put the following into Spanish, using the prompt in brackets.

Ejemplo: a Quiero comprar este jersey.

a Quiero comprar .... jersey. (*this*)

b ¿Cuánto cuesta .... camisa? (*that*)

c ¿Ves .... pantalón? (*that over there*)

d ¿La corbata roja? Sí, (*that one*).

e ¿Le gustan los sombreros? (*those ones*).

f Busco sandalias (*those ones, over there*).

Going out, TV and films

- Revise making arrangements to meet.

- Give your opinion on TV programmes and films.

A Invitations

SPEAK

Learn time phrases with **el**, **por**, **de**.

 When arranging to go out, you may need to mention:

- a day (e.g. on Friday)

- a specific time (e.g. at 11a.m.)

- a general time of day (e.g. the morning)

remember >>

Other useful time phrases are: *esta mañana* (this morning), *esta tarde* (this afternoon/evening) and *esta noche* (tonight).

Day of the week: use **el**	¿Quieres salir el viernes? *Do you want to go out on Friday?*
General time of day: use **por**	Te llamo por la tarde, ¿vale? *I'll ring you in the afternoon, OK?*
Specific time of day: use **de**	¿Nos vemos a las diez de la noche? *Shall we meet at 10 p.m?*

2 **Rellena cada espacio con el, por o de.** *Fill each gap with el, por or de.*

Javi:	¡Oye, Marifé! Soy Javi. ¿Quieres ir al cine conmigo ...**(1)**... viernes?
Marifé:	Lo siento. Tengo que ir al centro con Alicia a las dos ...**(2)**... la tarde.
Javi:	Vamos todos a la discoteca el sábado ...**(3)**... la noche – ¿quieres venir?
Marifé:	Lo siento. Tengo que cuidar a mi hermano. ¿Estás libre ...**(4)**... domingo?
Javi:	...**(5)**... la tarde solamente.
Marifé:	No sé. Voy a hablar con mamá. Te llamo mañana ...**(6)**... la mañana, ¿vale?

3 **Inventa otra conversación. Utiliza estos detalles.** *Invent another conversation. Use these details.*

- Javi invites Marifé to the bowling alley. She can't go, as she's going to the swimming pool.

- Javi suggests the ice-rink but Marifé has to look after her sister.

- Javi is only free on Sunday night, so Marifé promises to ring him in the afternoon.

remember >>

Revise phrases which indicate your opinion or point of view: see page 42.

READ

You need to be able to give your own view, both positive and negative.

¿Cuál es la opinión de cada persona? Escribe P (positiva), N (negativa) o P+N (positiva y negativa).
What is the opinion of each person? Write P (positive), N (negative), or P+N (positive and negative).

Ejemplo:

| Miguel | P | | Alicia | | | Santiago | |

| Belén | | | Pablo | | | Teresa | | | Eduardo | |

> Creo que las películas románticas son emocionantes. Vi 'Chocolate' la semana pasada, y me gustó mucho el ambiente.
> **Miguel**

> ¿Los dibujos animados? En general son divertidos, pero a veces son tontos.
> **Alicia**

> Creo que las comedias son buenas. Me gusta mucho el humor.
> **Santiago**

> En mi opinión, las películas de ciencia-ficción son estupendas. Vi la serie 'Stars Wars' hace poco, y lo mejor fueron los efectos especiales.
> **Belén**

> Las películas del oeste son malas. A veces el paisaje es bonito, pero los protagonistas no son interesantes.
> **Pablo**

> Pienso que las películas de aventuras son emocionantes, pero lo peor es la violencia.
> **Teresa**

> Los programas deportivos no me interesan mucho.
> **Eduardo**

>> practice questions

Write a short paragraph in Spanish about TV programmes or films you like or dislike, and say why. Include a brief account of a film you've seen recently. Use the comments above, and the following phrases, to help.

me gustan/encantan	*I like/love*
no me gustan/odio	*I don't like/hate*
Vi una película de acción que se llama … .	*I saw an action film called … .*
Fui al cine (el sábado pasado).	*I went to the cinema (last Saturday).*
Fue/era muy (emocionante).	*It was very (exciting).*
lo mejor/peor fue …	*the best/worst was …*

remember >>

Adjectives need to agree with the noun they describe: *las películas del oeste son aburridas, las comedias son divertidas.*

Popular culture

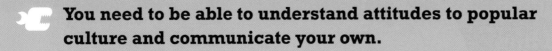

- You need to be able to understand attitudes to popular culture and communicate your own.

- This can include a wide range of issues: e.g. the media, fashion, celebrities, music.

- Explain what you spend money on.

A The media and celebrities

study hint >>

Words beginning 'in' (e.g. *infeliz*) often start with 'un' in English. The letters '-*dad*' at the end of a Spanish word are frequently '-ity' in English.

>> **key fact** If you read longer texts slowly and carefully, you will realize they are not as daunting as at first sight! Many unfamiliar words may be similar to English ones.

READ

Read the views below. Then answer the questions in English.

1 Which types of media does Martín mention? Name three.

2 What happens, according to Martín, as the result of wanting to imitate a star?

3 Apart from giving information, what else does Tere think the media do?

4 What do reality shows do, according to Tere?

5 What does Nuria say the whole world is like?

6 Which details do the stars give us about their lives, according to Nuria? Name two.

7 What do 40 per cent of young people want, according to one survey?

8 The cult of celebrity is like a religion, says David. In which ways? Name two.

> Los medios de comunicación son reponsables del culto a la celebridad. Los famosos están por todas partes – en la tele, en la radio, en la prensa, en las películas … Quieres imitar a tu estrella o ser como ella, pero no eres bastante delgada, ni guapa, ni rica. ¿La consecuencia? Eres infeliz y estàs descontenta con tu vida. Es un nuevo desorden psicológico.
> **Martín**

> Según una encuesta, el cuarenta por ciento de los jóvenes quieren ser famosos. El culto a la celebridad es una nueva religión. Primero, hay figuras sagradas (la gente famosa), luego los rituales (las giras* musicales, la entrega* de los Oscar) y, finalmente, eres miembro de una comunidad que adora y venera a sus 'estrellas'.
> **David**

> Los medios no existen simplemente para informar, sino también para entretener. Me gustan los 'reality shows', como 'Gran Hermano' o 'España Tiene Talento'. No tratan siempre de gente famosa. Estos programas celebran las personalidades y los talentos de la gente común.
> **Tere**

> Hoy en día, el mundo entero es un mercado. Los famosos son mercancía, y nosotros los consumidores. Ellos venden fotos y detalles íntimos de sus bodas, sus niños, sus relaciones – y nosotros los compramos en revistas y en programas de la tele. No es un bueno uso de los medios.
> **Nuria**

* gira *tour*,
* entrega *presentation*

B Fashion

>> **key fact** Learn verb endings. They give you the information about who is speaking.

READ

1. Look carefully in a text at what the writer is saying about him/herself: **yo** ... *(I ...)*, **me gusta** *(I like)*.

2. Don't be misled by how the verb is describing what others are doing: **mis amigos** ... *(my friends)*, **otras personas** ... *(other people)*.

Lee lo que escribe Amalia, y elige la frase correcta a, b, o c. *Read what Amalia says and choose the correct phrase a, b, or c.*

1 En cuanto a ropa, Amalia ...
   a gasta mucho dinero
   b gasta poco
   c no gasta nada

2 Al instituto, le gusta llevar ...
   a ropa sport
   b ir a la moda
   c ropa cómoda

3 No le gustan las prendas de ...
   a algodón
   b cuero
   c nilón

4 Prefiere llevar colores ...
   a oscuros
   b claros
   c vivos

5 Si va a una fiesta, prefiere la ropa ...
   a original
   b elegante
   c de marca

6 Compra en ...
   a los grandes almacenes
   b las tiendas pequeñas
   c el mercado

1 A mí no me interesa mucho la moda. Mis padres me dan dinero para comprar ropa, pero no gasto mucho.

2 Cuando voy al colegio, llevo vaqueros y un jersey o una camisa. Algunos de mis amigos siempre van a la moda, o llevan ropa sport (chandal, con zapatillas de deporte), pero yo no.

3 Algunos chicos de mi clase llevan telas sintéticas, como el nilón o el poliéster, pero yo prefiero las naturales, como el lino, el algodón o el cuero.

4 Soy morena, y por eso me van bien los colores alegres, como el rojo y el amarillo – no me gustan los colores tristes como el negro o el marrón, ni los aburridos como el azul claro o el color rosa.

5 No suelo llevar prendas de marca y no soy muy original tampoco. Para salir con amigos o ir a una fiesta, me gusta ponerme una falda larga y una chaqueta.

6 Cuando voy de compras, me gusta mirar los escaparates de los grandes almacenes, o ver lo que hay en el mercado, pero normalmente encuentro lo que busco en las boutiques.

>> practice questions

SPEAK/READ

Prepare your views on the following aspects of popular culture. Use and adapt the texts above to help.

- what I like/dislike wearing and why
- what I wear to school
- my views on fashion
- **Popular culture**
- media – too concerned with celebrities?
- positive aspects of the media

Shopping

A Buying a present

>> **key fact** Your speaking assessment may include a role-play situation, with bullet points to suggest what to say.

SPEAK

Read the conversation below, practise it with a friend, and invent others using the prompts in brackets.

A	Buenos días. ¿Qué desea?
B	¡Buenos días! Estoy buscando **un regalo** para mi abuela. *(Name item)*
A	Mmm… vamos a ver. ¿Le gusta este plato?
B	Sí, me gusta **el diseño** y es **muy bonito**. *(Say what you like about it)*. **Pero me parece un poco caro**. *(Mention a problem/something you don't like)*
A	¿Cuánto quiere gastarse?
B	**Entre diez y quince euros**, pero no más. *(Explain how much you want to pay)*
A	Este jarrón es muy bonito, ¿no?
B	**Sí. Pero es un poco frágil**, creo. *(Mention a difficulty/problem)*
A	¿Se lo puedo envolver bien en plástico con burbujas*, si quiere?
B	Lo dejo, gracias … *(Say you'll leave it)*
A	De acuerdo.
B	¿Puedo ver **ese abanico** allí en el escaparate? *(Enquire about another item)*
A	¿Éste? Es precioso … ¿Le gusta?
B	Es **perfecto**. Gracias. *(Give your opinion)*
A	¿Lleva mucho tiempo aquí en España?
B	**Llegué el sábado pasado**. *(Say how long you've been here)* **Estoy aquí de intercambio**. *(Give reason for your visit)*
A	¿Le gusta España?
B	**Sí, ¡me encanta! Todo el mundo es muy simpático**, *(Give your opinion)* **y el paisaje es muy bonito**. *(Say something complimentary)*
A	Y ¿qué ha visto ya?
B	**El domingo hicimos una excursión a la** *(Say what you did, use past tense)* **montaña para ver los pueblos blancos y comimos en un restaurante muy típico en el campo**.
A	¡Qué bien! ¿Cuándo tiene que volver a casa?
B	**Volveremos a Gran Bretaña el martes** *(say what you will do, use future tense)* **que viene** y ¡con muy buenos recuerdos!
A	¡Me alegro!* Bueno, aquí tiene su abanico …

study hint >>

You can prepare for the unexpected by thinking around the situation: what would be natural or likely here? The questions will often give you the chance to use the past, future or conditional tense.

* plástico con burbujas – *bubble wrap*
* me alegro – *I'm glad*

B Stores guides

>> **key fact** Don't forget to revise tourist topics you covered some time ago – they may come up in the reading or listening.

READ

You will need to be able to understand stores guides and names of shops. Choose the correct floor and section for each item on the teenager Jordi's list.

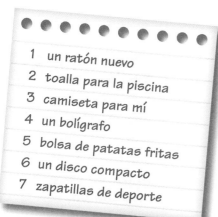

1 un ratón nuevo
2 toalla para la piscina
3 camiseta para mí
4 un bolígrafo
5 bolsa de patatas fritas
6 un disco compacto
7 zapatillas de deporte

Guía de departamentos

6	Agencia de Viajes – Restaurante - Cafetería
5	Oportunidades - Hogar Textil - Muebles
4	Informática - Deporte - Artículos de Viaje
3	Juguetería - Imagen y Sonido - Tienda de Música
2	Confección caballeros - Confección bebés - Niños
I	Confección señoras - Moda Joven - Zapatería - Bolsos
PB	Joyería - Complementos - Perfumería - Regalos
S	Supermercado – Droguería – Electrodomésticos - Jardín

C Local and out-of-town shopping

READ

Where do the teenagers 1–8 like to shop: in their local area, in a shopping centre out of town, or they don't mind?

Escribe la letra correcta para cada persona.
Write the correct letter for each person.

1 Prefiero comprar en las tiendas cerca de casa porque no tengo transporte.

2 Me gustar comprar todo en un edificio – es más fácil.

3 Como me no interesan mucho las compras, compro donde puedo.

4 Con todo en un lugar, ahorras tiempo y el surtido de productos es más grande.

5 Están abiertas sin interrupción y es fácil aparcar. En mi barrio, eso es imposible.

6 Los grandes almacenes en las afueras quitan clientes a las tiendas pequeñas del centro. No voy nunca.

7 La calle principal ahora tiene más tiendas con fines benéficos que cualquier otra calle. ¿Por qué? Tenemos un nuevo centro comercial a dos kilómetros. Lo odio.

8 Voy donde hay mejores precios y gangas. No me importa dónde compro.

	A en mi barrio	B centro comercial en las afueras	C me da igual
1			

>> practice questions

SPEAK/WRITE

Write a paragraph about where you like to shop and why. Describe something you bought recently. Use the phrases from C above to help.

Holiday activities

 Understand information in restaurants and cafés.

 Exchange information and opinions about holidays.

A On holiday

 **Watch out for negatives: they can change the meaning.**

READ

This next activity tests your ability to understand negatives and opposites.

Revise **no ... nada** (*nothing*), **no ... nunca** (*never*), **no ... nadie** (*no-one*).

Take particular care with sentences 3, 5 and 7.

Elige la palabra correcta para cada frase.
Choose the correct word for each sentence.

1 Teresa está de vacaciones con sus ....

2 El hotel es ....

3 La playa no está ....

4 La comida es ....

5 En general, no hace .... tiempo.

6 No llueve ....

7 Como deporte, le gusta hacer ....

> **remember >>**
>
> Negatives like *nunca*, *nadie*, *nada* can also come at the start of a sentence, in which case they lose the *no*.

> ¡Hola! ¿Qué tal? Estoy aquí de vacaciones con mamá y papá. El hotel es precioso y grande, y está cerca de la playa. Me gusta la comida – está muy rica. A veces hace viento, pero en general hace calor, y nada de lluvia – ¡qué bien! Juego al voleibol en la playa y nado en la piscina. A veces voy de compras en el pueblo, que es muy antiguo. El sábado voy a ir de excursión a la montaña.
>
> Teresa

hermanos   buena   equitación   bonito   mucho   padres   cerca   mal   nunca   lejos   cómodo   natación

B Using different tenses

SPEAK/WRITE

In a speaking or a writing assessment about an exchange visit or holiday, you may be given some points to guide you. Try this activity in preparation. Tell Teresa:

1 Where you are spending your holidays (*in Scotland*).

2 What the town is like (*pretty, touristy*).

3 What you are doing (*visiting castles, walking on beach/coast*).

4 What the weather is like (*quite warm, rains sometimes*).

5 What you did yesterday (*hired a bike*).

6 What you are going to do at the weekend (*go on a boat trip*).

> **remember >>**
>
> If you are aiming for higher grades, make sure you use past, present and future tenses.

READ

Make sure you know a range of common dishes and foods.

1 You read the following menu in a restaurant window.

¿Qué se puede comer? Escribe ✔ en 4 casillas.
What can you eat? Put a ✔ in 4 boxes.

Menú del día
Gazpacho andaluz
Ensaladilla rusa
Zumos
✳✳✳
Hamburguesa con queso
Tortilla española
Filete de ternera
✳✳✳
Piña en almíbar
Flan
Tarta de limón con nata

1	pescado	☐
2	carne	☐
3	huevos	☐
4	legumbres	☐
5	helados	☐
6	fruta	☐
7	dulces	☐

remember >>

If the instruction asks you to tick four boxes, do tick four even if you're not sure – there aren't any marks for leaving a blank space.

2 Revise phrases for ordering food and drink.

Explica lo que quieres comer y beber. *Explain what you want to eat and drink.*

Camarero/a:	Buenas tardes, señores. ¿Qué van a tomar?
Tú:	De primero, quiero …
Camarero/a:	¿Y de segundo?
Tú:	Me gustaría probar …
Camarero/a:	¿Y de postre?
Tú:	Para mí …
Camarero/a:	¿Y para beber?
Tú:	Quisiera …

tomato salad

Spanish omelette and chips

strawberry ice cream

fizzy mineral water

>> practice questions

You have just finished an exchange visit to Spain.

Write an article in Spanish (about 120–150 words) for their regional magazine.

- **con quién fuiste y cómo**
- **cuánto tiempo te quedaste**
- **lo que visitaste**
- **alguna excursión que hiciste**
- **tu opinión de tu estancia en España**
- **lo que quieres hacer el año próximo**

exam tip >>

Make sure you use tenses in the past, future and present tenses. Add descriptive adjectives, and opinions to improve marks for quality of language.

Vocabulary

A Accommodation

Quisiera reservar …/Hice una reserva.	*I'd like to reserve …/I made a reservation.*
¿Tiene habitaciones libres … ?	*Have you any free rooms … ?*
¿Para cuántas noches/personas?	*For how many nights/people?*
para esta noche, para (6) noches	*for tonight, for (6) nights*
del (5) al (11) de agosto	*from the (5th) to the (11th) of August*
¿El desayuno está incluido?	*Is breakfast included?*
¿A qué nombre?	*And your name?/In which name?*
¿A qué hora se sirve (la cena)?	*What time is (dinner) served?*
¿Tiene balcón/vistas al mar?	*Does it have a balcony/a sea view?*
¿Hay sitio para (una tienda familiar)?	*Is there room/space for (a family tent)?*
¿Dónde se puede (aparcar)?	*Where can you (park)?*
¿Quiere firmar la ficha, por favor?	*Can you sign the form, please?*

un ascensor	*the lift*	(el) saco de dormir	*sleeping bag*
una habitación	*a room*	… no funciona	*… isn't working*
doble, individual	*double, single*	(la) llave, (la) luz	*the key, the light*
con tres camas	*with three beds*	no hay (jabón)	*there's no (soap)*
con ducha/baño	*with shower/bath*	papel higiénico	*toilet paper*
pensión completa	*full board*	(la) pasta de dientes	*toothpaste*
media pensión	*half board*	un secador de pelo	*hairdryer*

B On the phone

¿Está …? ¿Me pone con …?	*Is … there? Can I speak to …?*
¿De parte de quién? De parte de …	*Who's speaking? It's …*
Está comunicando. No contesta.	*It's busy. It's not answering.*
¿Cuál es el número/prefijo?	*What's the number/dialling code?*
¿Qué número hay que marcar?	*What number do you have to dial?*
¿Puedo dejar un recado?	*Can I leave a message?*
un número equivocado	*a wrong number*
en línea, en contacto con	*on the line, in communication with*
¿Tiene una agenda de teléfonos?	*Have you got a phone book?*
Voy a dejar un mensaje en el contestador	*I'm going to leave a voicemail*
a la atención de, enviado por	*for the attention of, sent by*
enviar/recibir un mensaje de texto	*to send/receive a text message*
llamar, colgar, marcar	*to call, to hang up, to dial*
dejar, hablar (con)	*to leave, to speak (with)*

Grammar

C The perfect tense

The perfect tense indicates what has happened, e.g. 'I've lost …' (my key); 'I've left my bag on the bus'; 'I've eaten seafood'. To form this tense, you will need two parts:

THE PERFECT TENSE				IRREGULARS	
-ar (dejar)	(yo) he	dej**ado**	I've left	escrito	(written)
				hecho	(done/made)
-er (comer)	(yo) he	com**ido**	I've eaten	puesto	(put on)
				muerto	(died) (el/ella ha)
-ir (salir)	(yo) he	sal**ido**	I've left	roto	(broken)
			I've gone out	visto	(seen)

Other forms you might need are:

- **Tú has (dejado)**, etc. *You have (left)*, etc.

- **Él, ella, usted ha (dejado),** etc. *He/she has, you have (left)*, etc.

> ### study hint >>
> *Dejar* (to leave) indicates leaving an object or a person behind.

Work out the correct part of the verb in Spanish to go in the gaps below. The infinitive is in brackets.

Ejemplo: 1 ¿Has visitado el sur de España?

1 (visitar) ¿ _____ el sur de España?   *Have you visited the south of Spain?*

2 (perder) ¿_____ tu pasaporte?   *You've lost your passport?*

3 (probar) Sí, _____ la tortilla española.   *Yes, I've tried Spanish omelette.*

4 (salir) ¿Irene? _____ hace poco.   *Irene? She went out a little while ago.*

5 (dejar) Él _____ su dinero en casa.   *He has left his money at home.*

D The gerund and continuous tenses

The gerund in English ends in -ing, e.g. walking, reading. It's often used with while, when, by: when walking to school … while eating … by writing … Form it like this:

-ar verbs	*remove* -ar	-ando	*add* andar - andando *(walking)*
-er verbs	*remove* -er	-iendo	*add* comer - comiendo *(eating)*
-ir verbs	*remove* -ir	-iendo	*add* escribir - escribiendo *(writing)*

The present continuous indicates what you are doing right now (I'm studying) and the imperfect tense describes what you were doing (I was watching TV when …). Use the present (p. 5) or imperfect (p. 71) tense of the verb estar and the gerund.

¿Yo? Estoy haciendo mis deberes.	*Me? I'm doing my homework.*
Cuando llegué, María estaba planchando.	*When I arrived, María was ironing.*
Paso muchas horas navegando por Internet.	*I spend many hours surfing the net.*
Estábamos comiendo cuando llegó Tere.	*We were eating when Tere arrived.*

Accommodation

A Enquiring about facilities

WRITE

Revise how to ask questions as well as answer them.

You may have to book into a hotel or take the role of receptionist. This activity reminds you of useful words and phrases.

Rellena los espacios. *Fill in the gaps.*

Ejemplo: ¿El Hotel Malibú?

¿El ...**(1)**... Malibú?

¿Hay una ...**(2)**... cubierta?

¿La ...**(3)**... está lejos?

¿Puedo reservar una ...**(4)**... individual?

¿La habitación tiene ...**(5)**...?

¿Hay ...**(6)**... en la habitación?

Para cuatro noches, del ...**(7)**... al dieciséis de septiembre.

Voya traer mi ...**(8)**... portátil. ¿Hay conexión Wi-Fi?

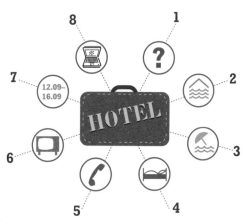

B Handling a phone conversation

Take the part of receptionist in the dialogue below. Use full sentences and be courteous!
You will need to use the formal 'you' (**usted**) with verbs.

1	¡Hola!	Hotel Jardín Tropical	(Hotel Jardín Tropical).
2	¿El Hotel Jardín Tropical en Tenerife?	....	(Yes. How can I help you?)
3	Quisiera hacer una reserva para dos personas.	....	(When, and for how long?)
4	Para seis noches, del siete al trece.	....	(Fine. Type of room?)
5	Una habitación doble, con baño.	....	(No problem. Name?)
6	Yo me apellido Pérez, y mi mujer se apellida Thompson.	....	(Spell it, please?)
7	T-H-O-M-P-S-O-N.	....	(I've got it now, thank you.)
8	¿Qué servicios tiene para los usuarios de Internet?	....	(Wi-fi in the sitting area.)
9	¿Y si no tengo mi propio ordenador?	....	(Special computer room, open 24 hrs.)
10	Perfecto.		

C Making a letter of complaint

>> **key fact** Knowing your grammar will help with understanding and writing letters or emails.

1. The following task will help you focus on verb endings. Choose the correct verb for each gap in the email letter below.

2. Study the verbs on the list first. Work out the tense and who is doing the action – the verb endings give you this information, e.g. **Somos** is the **nosotros** *(we)* form.

3. Check your knowledge of tenses: present (p. 5), preterite (p. 48), imperfect (p. 71), future (p. 27, 70), conditional (p. 70).

Muy señor mío:

Somos la familia Brown de Londres, en Inglaterra. Durante las vacaciones de Semana Santa pasada, …(1)… uno de los chalés de su camping, del once al dieciocho de abril. Cuando …(2)… la reserva, usted nos aseguró* que el chalé tipo unifamiliar …(3)… ideal para nuestra familia de cinco personas. Este no fue el caso. …(4)… solamente camas para cuatro personas, y mi hija tuvo que dormir en el sofá. Cuando hablamos con la recepcionista, nos prometió una cama plegable, que nunca llegó. Además, la calefacción no …(5)… bien, y la ventana de la cocina no cerraba bien tampoco, así que entraba mucho frío. Intentamos hablar con usted personalmente varias veces, pero nunca fue 'el momento adecuado', según su recepcionista. Tuvimos que comprar un calentador en el pueblo, lo que nos …(6)… dinero y resultó en gastos elevados en nuestro consumo de electricidad. Nuestros tres hijos …(7)… a casa resfriados.

Fue una experiencia triste e innecesaria. Su camping …(8)… situado en un lugar precioso, con un paisaje maravilloso; todo estaba muy bien ordenado, y las instalaciones eran impecables. La única mejora que …(9)… sugerir es un lugar especial donde se puede atar* a los perros que, de momento, corren libremente por el parque infantil y a veces aterrorizan a los niños pequeños.

De momento no sabemos si …(10)… a su camping – eso depende de la respuesta que recibamos de usted.
En espera de su pronta respuesta, le saludamos atentamente.
Sr. y Sra. Brown

A	costó
B	había
C	sería
D	hicimos
E	volveremos
F	alquilamos
G	funcionaba
H	llegaron
I	está
J	podemos

*asegurar *to assure, reassure*, *atar *to tie up*

>> practice questions

WRITE

Write a letter complaint to a campsite, hotel or youth hostel. Include the following information:

- who you are and when you stayed

- what the problem was and why it caused a difficulty for you/your family

- what you liked about the place/area you stayed in

- suggest an improvement that could be made and why.

Services

Explain that someone else is not feeling well, and say what is wrong.

Talk or write about a loss or theft when on holiday.

A Parts of the body

WRITE

Revise the Spanish for the parts of the body.

 If you're ill, you'll need to be able to explain what is wrong with you.

 How many parts of the body do you know?

Completa cada palabra con las letras que faltan.
Complete each word with the letters which are missing.

1	la cab _ _ _	(head)	**8**	la espal _ _	(back)
2	la nar _ _	(nose)	**9**	el bra _ _	(arm)
3	los oíd _ _	(ears)	**10**	la ma _ _	(hand)
4	la boc _	(mouth)	**11**	el de _ _	(finger)
5	la mu _ _ _	(back tooth)	**12**	el estóm _ _ _	(stomach)
6	la garg _ _ _ _	(throat)	**13**	la pie _ _ _	(leg)
7	los oj _ _	(eyes)	**14**	el pi _	(foot)

Remember: with **el/la**, use **me duele**, e.g. '**Me duele la cabeza.**' With **los/las**, use **me duelen**, e.g. '**Me duelen los pies.**'

B Explaining what's the matter

SPEAK

You may have to take part in a role-play where you are feeling ill.

Sustituye las expresiones en negrita por otras apropiadas.
Replace the expressions in bold by other appropriate ones.

+	¿Qué tal estás?
*	**No me encuentro bien**.
+	¿Qué te pasa?
*	Me duele **la garganta**.
+	¿Desde hace cuánto tiempo no te sientes bien?
*	**Desde ayer**.
+	¿Tienes otros síntomas?
*	Tengo **catarro** también.
+	Vamos a ver ...

la cabeza
no me siento bien
desde hace dos días
no estoy muy bien
el estómago
náuseas
fiebre
desde anoche

exam tip >>

Further back in time than yesterday needs *desde hace*, e.g. *No me siento bien desde hace dos días*. (I haven't been feeling well for two days.)

>> key fact

You need to be able to use past tenses in speaking/writing.

READ

1 Explaining you've lost an item usually involves a range of tenses: where you lost it, what it was like, when you will be returning home.

2 Though the language may be more complex, the task might be quite simple.

3 Study carefully what you have to do. The activity below simply asks you to tick the pictures which reflect what happened.

Escribe ✔ en cada casilla apropiada. *Put a ✔ in each appropriate box.*

> Me llamo Martine Josef, y soy de Limoges, en Francia.

> Estoy aquí de vacaciones – llegué el 15 de julio, y vuelvo el 22. He perdido mi bolsa en la estación de tren. Creo que la dejé en los servicios.

> Es de cuero negro, tipo mochila, y contenía mi monedero, mi pasaporte, y las llaves de la casa donde me alojo.

> No sé cuánto vale - creo que unos 15 euros. Pero había 30 euros en mi monedero.

1 ☐
2 ☐
3 ☐
4 ☐

5 ☐
6 ☐
7 ☐
8 ☐

>> practice questions

WRITE

As part of a writing assessment about your holidays, write a paragraph in Spanish explaining:

* that you lost an item
* describe its colour and size
* explain what it contained
* say where/how you lost it
* say how much it was worth.

exam tip >>

Use the perfect tense to say what you have lost: (*he perdido*), the preterite to indicate what happened: (*Perdí mi bolsa en el bar.*), and the imperfect to describe what it was like: (*era*) or what it contained (*contenía*).

Staying in touch

 You may need to understand, respond to or leave a phone message.

 You may be asked to give your opinion on mobile phones.

A Phone messages

SPEAK

 You may hear, or have to give, a phone message.

 Revise useful phrases by doing the activity below.

Empareja a–h con 1–8. *Match a–h with 1–8.*

1 Hotel Santa Fé, ¿dígame?

2 Sí. ¿En qué puedo servirle?

3 Un momento ... Lo siento, está comunicando.

4 ¿Quiere dejar algún recado?

5 A las cinco. Muy bien. ¿De parte de quién?

6 ¿Cuál es su número de teléfono, señor Brown?

7 ¿Y cuál es el prefijo de la ciudad?

8 Muchas gracias, señor. Se lo diré.

> **remember >>**
>
> Spanish phone numbers are given in pairs: 54 20 12 is *cincuenta y cuatro, veinte, doce.* Where there is a group of three at the start (e.g. 430), the first one is given on its own: *cuatro, treinta ...*

a Soy Jason Brown, de Inglaterra.

b Es el 62 42 98.

c Muchas gracias. Hasta luego.

d Vale. ¿Me puede llamar a las cinco?

e Buenas tardes. ¿Hablo con la recepcionista?

f ¡Vaya! ¡Qué fastidio!

g Es el 0161.

h ¿Me pone con la señorita Jiménez, por favor?

Now practise another dialogue: the receptionist's replies remain mostly the same, but you need to give the following information:

- Ask if you're talking to the secretary.
- Ask to be put through to Sr. Gómez.
- Express your annoyance.
- Ask him to call you at half past four.
- Explain you're Sam Thompson, from Wales.
- Give her your phone number: 740692.
- Give her the code: 01745.
- Say 'thank you' and 'goodbye'.

> **remember >>**
>
> To express anger or disappointment, you can use *¡Qué pena!, ¡Qué fastidio!, ¡Qué lata!*

>> key fact

Attitudes and feelings are not always expressed directly.

READ

1 Read carefully and work out the meaning of what is being said in the view below.

2 Take a step back and listen to the tone or emotion behind what they are saying.
For each person A–G, choose the correct attitude. There will be one left over.

A	Ahora que tengo un teléfono móvil, mis padres siempre pueden ponerse en contacto conmigo. Les da un sentimento de seguridad a ellos y a mí también.
B	¡No entiendo cómo la gente se mantenía en contacto antes de los móviles! ¿Qué hacían?
C	Es el ruido de los móviles lo que me molesta sobre todo – o, mejor, es la gente insensible a las necesidades de los demás. Me hace subirme por las paredes.
D	Si no tienes un móvil como yo, o tus padres no te dejan tenerlo, eres la excepción. La gente de mi clase me ignora y es difícil hacer amigos.
E	Cuando ocurren desastres los móviles son muy útiles. Hay gente que está viva hoy porque llamaron a los servicios de emergencia desde sus móviles. Por eso me preocupo si no llevo el móvil en el bolsillo.
F	Los móviles consumen dinero. Yo tengo una tarjeta prepago, y uso mi móvil solamente cuando es necesario. Suelo llamar por el telefono fijo*.
G	Como siempre pierdo mi cargador* ¡no uso mucho el móvil!

* fijo - *fixed* * el cargador - *phone charger*

1	careless	**3**	lonely	**5**	curious	**7**	irritated
2	delighted	**4**	careful	**6**	anxious	**8**	safe

3 Re-read the views and answer these questions in English. Write the appropriate letter.
Who …

a finds himself excluded in school?

b uses a landline more?

c does not have a mobile?

d refers to the noise of mobiles?

e mentions natural disasters?

f talks about the era before mobiles phones?

>> practice questions

SPEAK

Prepare your answers to these questions:

¿Cuáles son las ventajas de los móviles?

¿Tienes tú un teléfono móvil?

¿Cuáles son los inconvenientes?

¿Cómo lo usas?

Listening section C

You will need to use the CD-ROM to complete this section.

A Leisure

>> **key fact** Listen carefully to the endings of words – it can make all the difference! (e.g. *chico* – boy, *chica* – girl).

1 Jaime talks about his trip to the cinema. Tick the correct box.

A	When	
1	during the week	
2	last night	
3	last weekend	

B	With	
1	older brother	
2	younger brother	
3	younger sister	

C	Film was...	
1	fun	
2	boring	
3	exciting	

2 Listen and tick the appropriate box for each activity 1–5.

		Likes	Dislikes	Doesn't say
1	action films			
2	romantic films			
3	books			
4	music			
5	dancing			

> **exam tip >>**
>
> Mentally revise expressions of liking/disliking before you start.

B Illness

>> **key fact** Read the sentences carefully before you start, so you know what to focus on.

You hear this conversation in your exchange partner's home.

Put a tick in the three (3) correct boxes.

1	She feels sick.	
2	She has a headache.	
3	She'd like some tablets.	
4	She wants to go out this afternoon.	
5	She is going to sleep for a while.	
6	Her friend has got something planned this evening.	

C Eating out

>> **key fact** Make sure you write down the important pieces of information – only one word may be needed for the mark.

Listen and complete the sentences in English.

1 How many ......?

2 Would you like ......?

3 The prawns are ......

4 The bread is ......

5 There are no ...... left.

6 The service ......

7 The toilets are on the ...... floor.

8 They are ...... the phones.

D Shopping

>> **key fact** If there are picture symbols, first work out which Spanish words you might expect to hear. This will help to get your ear and brain tuned!

Choose the correct item(s) for each person. There are two for Roberto and one for Alicia. Write the number in the correct box.

Roberto ☐ ☐ Alicia ☐

E Accommodation

>> **key fact** Where you have more to write, make sure your English answer is specific and clear: e.g. not just 'hotel in bad position' but 'hotel 2 kilometres from the beach.'

Listen to the comments about the hotel. Write your answers in the spaces provided.

	Problems	
Rooms	1	....
	2	....
Food	1	....
	2	....

Vocabulary

¿Qué asignaturas estudias?		How many subjects do you study?	
Estudio (siete) en total.		I study (seven) altogether.	
(Cinco) obligatorias, y (dos) optativas.		(Five) compulsory, and (two) options.	
¿Cuáles son? Estudio (física ...)		What are they? I study (physics ...)	
¿Qué asignatura te gusta más/menos?		Which subject do you like best/least?	
¿Por qué te gusta/no te gusta?		Why do you like it/not like it?	
¿Cómo es tu instituto?		What's your school like?	
¿Qué instalaciones tiene?		What facilities does it have?	

la lengua	(English) language	las ciencias	sciences
la literatura	literature	la química	chemistry
el francés, el alemán	French, German	la biología, la ética	biology, PSHE
el español, la geografía	Spanish, geography	el arte dramático	drama
la historia	history	el comercio	business studies
la informática	IT, computing	el dibujo, el diseño	art, design
la tecnología	technology	las matemáticas	maths
las ciencias económicas	economics	los trabajos manuales	CDT
el idioma	language	la cocina, la física	cookery, physics

(des)obedecer	to (dis)obey	fracasar	to fail
apoyar, aprender	to support, to learn	golpear, insultar	to hit, to insult
aprobar, atacar	to pass, to attack	intimidar	to bully
callar(se)	to be quiet	levantar la mano	to raise one's hand
castigar	to punish	molestar, olvidar	to disturb, to forget
comenzar	to begin	pasar	to spend (time)
comprender	to understand	pedir permiso	to ask permission
contestar, dibujar	to answer, to draw	preguntar	to ask
diseñar	to design	prometer	to promise
escuchar, mirar	to listen, to look	repasar	to revise
enseñar	to teach	sacar (notas)	to get (marks)
entender, estudiar	to understand, to study	suspender	to fail, to suspend
faltar	to be absent	terminar	to finish, to end

desobediente	disobedient	obligatorio/a	obligatory
femenino/a	feminine, girls'	primario/a	primary, basic
estricto/a	strict	privado/a, público/a	private, public
difícil, fácil	difficult, easy	secundario/a	secondary
físico/a	physical	severo/a	severe
insolente	insolent, cheeky	sobresaliente	excellent
masculino/a	masculine, boys'	trabajador/a	hard-working
mixto/a	mixed	útil, inútil	useful, useless

el/la alumno/a	*pupil*	la letra, la nota	*letter, mark*
el apoyo, los apuntes	*support, notes*	el/la profesor/a	*teacher*
ausente, la ayuda	*absent, help*	el recreo	*break-time*
el bachillerato	*diploma*	la regla	*ruler, rule*
el castigo	*punishment*	el respeto	*respect*
el comportamiento	*behaviour*	la respuesta	*reply*
la conducta	*conduct, behaviour*	el resultado	*result*
la escuela	*primary school*	el resumen	*summary*
el/la estudiante	*student*	la tarea, el tema	*task, topic*
los estudios, el examen	*studies, exam*	el texto, el trabajo	*text, work*
el éxito, el fracaso	*success, failure*	el trimestre, el tutor	*term, tutor*
el intercambio	*exchange*	el uniforme	*uniform*
la lección	*lesson*	la víctima	*victim*

los aseos, un aula	*toilets, classroom*	los vestuarios	*cloakrooms*
una cantina/un comedor	*canteen*	un laboratorio	*laboratory*
un gimnasio	*gymnasium*	el salón de actos	*assembly hall*
una cancha de tenis	*tennis court*	el taller	*workshop*
un campo de deportes	*sports field*	una sala de profesores	*staff room*

B Part-time jobs

¿Tienes algún empleo? ¿Cuándo trabajas?	*Do you have a job? When do you work?*
Trabajo todos los días, el fin de semana, de/a	*I work every day, at the weekend, from/till*
¿Cuántas horas trabajas? Trabajo ...	*How many hours do you work? I work ...*
¿Cuándo empiezas/terminas? Empiezo/termino ...	*When do you start? finish? I start/finish ...*
¿Cuánto ganas? Gano ...	*How much do you earn? I earn ...*
¿Qué opinas del trabajo? Es (aburrido/pesado).	*What do you think about work? It's (boring).*

interesante, agradable	*interesting, pleasant*	rutinario, repetitivo	*routine, repetitive*
útil, difícil, fácil	*useful, difficult, easy*	bien/mal pagado, duro	*well/badly paid, hard*

C Education issues

¿Adónde quieres ir ...	*Where do you want to go ...*
para seguir tus/sus estudios?	* to continue your studies?*
Quiero/Espero ir a ...	*I want to/I hope to go to ...*
una academia, la universidad	* an academy, university*
hacer una carrera en ...	* to do a university course in ...*
¿Qué opinas de tener reglas/normas?	What do you think about having rules?
¿Estás a favor del uniforme?	Are you in favour of uniform?
tener la opción de	to have the option to
tener prácticas en, tener formacion en	to have work experince in, to have training in

Grammar

A The future and conditional tenses

The future tense indicates what will happen. The conditional indicates what would happen. You will notice that the endings are added to the infinitive. They are the same for all three verb types: **-ar**, **-er**, **-ir**. The examples below use **hablar** (to speak).

	FUTURE	CONDITIONAL
	-ar (hablar)	**-ar (hablar)**
yo	hablar**é**	hablar**ía**
tú	hablar**ás**	hablar**ías**
él, ella, usted	hablar**á**	hablar**ía**
nosotros/as	hablar**emos**	hablar**íamos**
vosotros/as	hablar**éis**	hablar**íais**
ellos, ellas, ustedes	hablar**án**	hablar**ían**

> **remember >>**
>
> **The future of *hay* (there is/are) is *habrá*, and the conditional is *habría*.**

Hablaré con el gerente mañana.	*I will speak to the manager tomorrow.*
Comeremos en la terraza.	*We will eat on the terrace.*
¿Dónde vivirías?	*Where would you live?*
¿Qué tipo de trabajo te gustaría?	*What sort of work would you like?*

The following verbs have irregular stems in both the future and the conditional. They have regular endings:

INFINITIVE		STEM	INFINITIVE		STEM
to say	decir	dir-	*to know*	saber	sabr-
to do, make	hacer	har-	*to go out*	salir	saldr-
to be able to	poder	podr-	*to have*	tener	tendr-
to put, lay, set	poner	pondr-	*to come*	venir	vendr-
to want to	querer	querr-	*to be worth*	valer	valdr-

Lo haré pasado mañana.	*I will do it the day after tomorrow.*
Tendrá que ir a Inglaterra en mayo.	*He will have to go to England in May.*
Querríamos viajar si es posible.	*We would like to travel, if possible.*
Podría ir a la universidad.	*I would be able to go to university.*

Put the underlined verbs into the future tense, and the verbs in brackets into the conditional.

¿El instituto del futuro? Creo que <u>tiene</u> menos alumnos jóvenes y más adultos. Todo el mundo <u>aprende</u> en centros de información, y no en aulas. <u>Hay</u> más ordenadores y <u>es</u> posible quedarse en casa. Si fuera posible, yo (ir) sólo un día o dos a la semana, y (poder) estudiar una mayor Variedad de asignaturas. (Querer) visitar más países, (hacer) más prácticas laborales ¡y no (haber) tantos exámenes!

The imperfect tense

The imperfect tense describes what something was like, what was happening, or what used to happen. For regular verbs, remove the **-ar**, **-er**, **-ir** from the infinitive, and add these endings:

	-ar hablar *(to speak)*	-er beber *(to drink)*	-ir vivir *(to live)*
yo	habl**aba**	beb**ía**	viv**ía**
tú	habl**abas**	beb**ías**	viv**ías**
él, ella, usted	habl**aba**	beb**ía**	viv**ía**
nosotros/as	habl**ábamos**	beb**íamos**	viv**íamos**
vosotros/as	habl**abais**	beb**íais**	viv**íais**
ellos, ellas, ustedes	habl**aban**	beb**ían**	viv**ían**

IR *(to go)*	iba, ibas, iba, íbamos, ibais, iban
SER *(to be)*	era, eras, era, éramos, erais, eran
VER *(to see)*	veía, veías, veía, veíamos, veíais, veían

Vivíamos en la costa. Era tranquilo.	*We used to live on the coast. It was quiet.*
Iba a la playa. Había mucha gente.	*I used to go to the beach. There were a lot of people.*
Hacía buen tiempo.	*The weather was good.*

Put the verbs in brackets into the imperfect tense.

Ejemplo: (ir) – iba

Hice mis prácticas laborales en la oficina de un arquitecto, igual que mi amigo Juan. Yo (ir) al trabajo andando, porque la oficina no (estar) muy lejos de casa, pero él (coger) el autobús. Nosotros (empezar) a las nueve, pero los otros empleados (tener) que estar allí a las ocho. Me (gustar) el trabajo: yo (archivar) primero, o (hacer) recados, y Juan (coger) el teléfono y (repartir) el correo. A la hora de comer, nosotros (soler) ir al bar de enfrente.

Verbs of obligation

There are several ways of expressing the idea of *having* to do something. Each of them are followed by the infinitive:

Tener que ... *(have to, must)*	Deber ... *(ought to, should)*	Hay que ... *(one has to)*

Tengo que hacerlo ahora.	*I have to do it now. (No choice!)*
Debo hacerlo ahora.	*I ought to do it now. (But I might decide not to.)*
Hay que trabajar mucho.	*One has to work hard. (Idea of necessity.)*

remember >>

Tener que has the same forms as *tener*. (See page 5 for the present tense, and page 48 for the preterite.) *Deber* is a regular verb.

School and after the exams

- Make sure you can say which subjects you study.

- Add your opinions, likes and dislikes about school.

- Explain what you're going to do after the exams.

A Likes and dislikes

READ

Check that you know different ways of expressing likes and dislikes: look again at page 13.

1. A common exam question type asks you to read a short passage, and then tick the sentences about it which are true.

2. Do not assume that all expressions of disliking or not liking have **no** in them. You can use **no me gusta nada** (*I don't like*), but also **odio/detesto** (*I hate*).

Escribe ✔ en las casillas si las frases son verdaderas. *Put a ✔ in the boxes beside the sentences below which are true.*

> ¡Hola!
>
> Me llamo Nuria. Mi colegio es grande: tiene más de mil alumnos. Es bastante nuevo, con muchas aulas, pasillos, laboratorios, un gimnasio, un salón de actos, una biblioteca, despachos para la administración y el director, dos cocinas, un patio y una cafetería. Mi asignatura favorita es la educación física, pero se me dan muy bien las ciencias también. No me gustan nada el inglés ni el francés porque son difíciles y aburridos; y odio la historia porque no saco nunca buenas notas. En general, no está mal mi instituto. Lo bueno es que tengo muchos amigos y los profesores son simpáticos.

1. El instituto de Nuria es pequeño. ☐

2. Su instituto no es muy antiguo. ☐

3. Le encanta hacer deporte. ☐

4. Le gusta mucho estudiar física, química y biología. ☐

5. Las lenguas no le interesan mucho. ☐

6. Nuria saca buenas notas en historia. ☐

7. Nuria está bastante contenta con su instituto. ☐

study hint >>

English, as a subject, is called *lengua y literature*, if it is your own language. If you want to talk about a foreign language, use *el idioma*, e.g. *Me gustan los idiomas, sobre todo el español.*

Make sure you can use the simple future tense: **voy a** ... (I'm going to ...)

1   You will need to prepare a few sentences on your plans for after the exams.

2   Use the grid below to do the role-play task. Put the English sentences into Spanish.

You are talking to your Spanish friend about your plans for the rest of the year.

¿Qué vas a hacer después de los exámenes?
(Say you're going to have a rest!)

¿Vas a quedarte en casa todo el verano?
(Say you'd also like to look for a job and earn some money.)

¿Y en septiembre?
(Explain that you're going to return to school and carry on studying.)

¿Vas a hacer más exámenes?
(Tell him/her that you hope to do do A-levels.)

Después de los exámenes, quiero ...	*descansar un tiempo.*
En verano, me gustaría .../voy a ...	*ir de vacaciones.*
	trabajar en mi ciudad.
	ganar dinero.
	pasarlo bien.
En septiembre, voy a ...	*volver al instituto.*
En el otoño, espero ...	*cambiar de instituto.*
	seguir estudiando.
	hacer Bachillerato.
	buscar un empleo.

study hint >>

The Spanish exam (*Bachillerato*) is the nearest equivalent to our A/S and A-level exams.

>> practice questions

In preparation for a speaking assessment or a written assessment about school and your plans for the future, write a short paragraph on each of the following:

* **las asignaturas que estudias**

* **la asignatura que te gusta más, y por qué**

* **una asignatura que no te gusta, y por qué**

* **tu colegio: lo bueno y lo malo**

* **qué vas a hacer depués de los exámenes**

study hint >>

Vocabulary and phrases you've used in one topic can be reused in another. Look back at pages 13–14 for more expressions of liking/disliking, page 68 for adjectives to describe your school, and pages 30–31 to say what is good and bad about it.

Part-time jobs

 Give and understand information about part-time jobs.

 Explain what you spend money on.

A Part-time jobs

READ

1. In the speaking assessment, you may want to talk about a part-time job, or work in the holidays.

2. You may be asked to explain what you do, your hours, how much you earn and what you think of it.

Para cada pregunta 1–7, escribe la letra de la respuesta apropiada. *For each question 1–7, write the letter of the appropriate reply.*

1 ¿Tienes algún empleo?	**a** Siete horas en total.
2 ¿Cuándo trabajas?	**b** Mis padres no me dejan trabajar.
3 ¿Cuántas horas trabajas?	**c** Sí, en un garaje.
4 ¿Cuándo empiezas?	**d** A las cuatro de la tarde.
5 ¿Cuándo terminas?	**e** Siete euros a la hora.
6 ¿Cuánto ganas?	**f** Los sábados.
7 ¿Qué opinas del trabajo?	**g** Es interesante. Aprendo mucho.
	h A las nueve de la mañana.

B Expanding your replies

>> key fact
Use verbs in your replies. It is good to say as much as you can.

SPEAK

1. In the replies a–h above, there are few verbs. Use a verb in each sentence: **trabajo** *(I work)*, **empiezo** *(I begin)*, **termino** *(I finish)*, **gano** *(I earn)*.

2. Use the information above to fill in the gaps below.

Rellena los espacios. *Fill in the gaps.*

¿Tienes algún empleo?

Sí. Trabajo en un garaje los ...**(1)**... . Trabajo ...**(2)**... horas normalmente: empiezo a las ...**(3)**... de la mañana, y termino a las ...**(4)**... de la tarde, por lo general.

¿Cuánto ganas?

Gano ...**(5)**... a la hora. No está mal, y me gusta el trabajo. Es duro y aburrido a veces, pero en general es ...**(6)**... .

 **study hint >>**

There will be an element of the unexpected in the assessment. Think around the topic: what else might you be asked here? For example, what might you like to do in the future? Is part-time work a good idea when you are studying? Prepare your replies.

READ

1. Reading texts and questions often contain 'false trails': similar words or expressions which can mislead unless you read other words around them carefully.

2. Each question 1–7 below has a 'false trail'. Read the following tips to help with the first three questions.

   Q1 contains the word numerosa, and text 1 has the numbers **dos** and **cinco**: don't be misled!

   Q2 The word **deportista** comes up in text 3, but are there any negatives near it? Who else does sport?

   Q3 The expression fin de semana appears in text 3, but is it in the context of weekend work?

Escribe el nombre de la persona más apropiada. *Write the name of the most appropriate person.*

¿Recibes dinero? ¿Cuánto? ¿Cuándo?

1 Mi madrastra es enfermera, y tiene que trabajar mucho. ¡Yo también! Cuido a mis hermanas (de dos y cinco años) los sábados y los domingos. Casi todo el dinero que gano lo uso para pagarme cursos de piragüismo.

Isabel

2 No me dan mucho dinero mis padres porque somos seis hermanos en total. Tampoco trabajo fuera de casa: tengo exámenes en junio. Cada noche tengo un montón de deberes – ¡demasiados!

Sabrina

3 Yo gano dinero trabajando en un garaje, de lunes a viernes. Empiezo a las seis de la tarde y termino a las diez de la noche. Gasto mi dinero en CD y revistas. No salgo mucho el fin de semana – estudio un poco – y no soy nada deportista.

Pablo

4 Mis padres me dan setenta euros al mes. Parece mucho, pero tengo que pagarme todo: la ropa, los libros, las diversiones, incluso los viajes en autobús para ir al instituto – ¡eso no es justo! A finales del mes, ¡no tengo ni un euro!

Enrique

1 ¿Quién es miembro de una familia numerosa? ....

2 ¿Quién es deportista? ....

3 ¿Quién tiene que trabajar el fin de semana? ....

4 ¿Quién gasta todo su dinero? ....

5 ¿Quién tiene que estudiar mucho? ....

6 ¿Quién no recibe dinero de sus padres? ....

7 ¿Quién prefiere quedarse en casa los fines de semana? ....

>> practice questions

Prepare to talk about part-time work and money. Use the points below.

- **¿Tienes algún empleo?**
- **¿Qué haces? ¿Dónde trabajas?**
- **¿Cómo es el horario?**
- **¿Cuánto dinero ganas/recibes?**
- **¿En qué gastas tu dinero?**
- **Recibes un aumento de sueldo. ¿En qué gastarías el dinero?**

study hint >>

The last prompt needs you to use the conditional tense (p. 70).

Education issues

- Prepare your thoughts on school issues: e.g. rules, uniform, benefits.

- Ensure you can talk or write about your choices of study and training.

A School: the good and the bad

>> **key fact** It is possible to find simple ways of explaining complex ideas: many expressions are similar to English ones.

SPEAK

1. You may be asked to give your opinion on different aspects of school life.

2. Choose the replies which most closely reflect your views from the alternatives below. Adapt them if you like.

Elige la respuesta más apropiada para ti. *Choose the reply which is most appropriate for you.*

¿Qué opinas de las reglas de tu instituto?
1 Creo que las reglas son ...
- necesarias.
- demasiado severas.
- estúpidas.

¿Por qué?
2 Las reglas existen para ...
- ayudarte a respetar los derechos de los demás.
- limitar tu libertad de expresión.
- fastidiar a los alumnos.

¿Hay algo que cambiarías?
3 Cambiaría las normas sobre ...
- el uniforme: sería mejor llevar lo que quieras.
- las asignaturas que se pueden estudiar.
- el castigo: no es justo.

¿Qué opinas de la disciplina en tu instituto?
4 Creo que ...
- es buena: la mayoría de los alumnos trabajan bien.
- es mala: hay mucha gente que no se comporta bien.
- puede ser mejor: algunos alumnos intimida a otros/a sus compañeros.

¿Cuáles son las ventajas de ir al instituto?
5 La ventaja más grande es que ...
- sales bien preparado/a.
- aprendes a relacionarte con muchas personas diferentes.
- puedes probar muchas asignaturas diferentes.

remember >>

Many Spanish words ending in *-ción* end in *-tion* in English, e.g. *atención, educación, acción.*

B Further study and training

READ

1 You may meet a task in which you have to tick two boxes for each question.

2 At a higher level, you need to read between the lines to judge likes, dislikes and feelings.

study hint >>

Practise reading longer items, with more complex language.

Escribe las letras correctas en las casillas. *Write the correct letters in the boxes.*

A Después de los exámenes de GCSE, quiero hacer un cursillo de formación profesional que se llama GNVQ. Hay más oportunidades para hacer prácticas en una oficina o en una compañía con este tipo de cursillo. No me interesa hacer algo muy académico. Pero si quiero, podré ir a la universidad después.

B Yo voy a pasar dos años estudiando para hacer los exámenes de A/S y A level. Es más o menos el equivalente español de Bachillerato. Normalmente se estudian tres o cuatro asignaturas. ¡Qué bien tener que estudiar sólo las asignaturas que te interesan!

C Tengo la intención de hacer los exámenes de A level en mi instituto. Es muy interesante estudiar una asignatura a fondo. Creo que es una buena preparación para los estudios universitarios que haré más tarde.

D En julio espero trabajar con mi tío, que es fontanero. Hacer nueve o diez años de estudios obligatorios es suficiente, ¡y no quiero hacer más! Mi tío me va a pagar cuatro días de la semana, y voy a ir a una escuela técnica los jueves para obtener los títulos profesionales necesarios.

1 ¿Quiénes piensan ir a la universidad?

2 ¿Quién va a ganar dinero?

3 ¿A quiénes les gusta estudiar?

4 ¿Quién está harto/a de estudiar?

5 ¿Quiénes van a trabajar y estudiar al mismo tiempo?

>> practice questions

WRITE/SPEAK

Prepare your replies to the following prompts. Make sure you use the past, present, future and conditional tenses and give your opinions.

Balancing part-time work and study

Best/worst job would be ...?

Work

Staying on at school: pros and cons

Plans for future study

Vocabulary

A Work experience

¿Dónde hiciste tus practicas laborales?	*Where did you do your work experience?*
Las hice en ... /Trabajé en ...	*I did it in .../I worked in ...*
¿Cuánto tiempo duraron? – Duraron ... días.	*How long did it last? – It lasted ... days.*
¿Cómo ibas a tu lugar de trabajo?	*How did you get to your workplace?*
Iba andando, en tren, en autobús.	*I used to go on foot, by train, by bus.*
¿Cuánto tiempo tardabas en llegar?	*How long did it take to get there?*
Tardaba unos (20) minutos.	*It took/used to take about (20) minutes.*
¿Cómo era el horario?	*What was your timetable like?*
Empezaba/terminaba a las (nueve).	*I began/I finished at (nine).*
¿Qué tenías que hacer?	*What did you have to do?*
Tenía que (archivar, coger el teléfono).	*I had to (do the filing, answer the phone).*

B Work, career and future plans

¿Qué planes tienes para el futuro?	*What plans have you got for the future?*
¿En qué te gustaría trabajar?	*What kind of work would you like to do?*
(No) Quiero ... preferiría ... tendré que ...	*I (don't) want ... I'd prefer ... I will have to ...*
ser (médico/a), tener que decidir	*to be (a doctor), to have to decide*
trabajar en el sector de (la industria)	*to work in (industry)*
tratar con (el público, los animales, los niños)	*to work with (the public, animals, children)*
tener un trabajo (científico, físico, artístico)	*to do a (scientific, physical, artistic) job*
¿En que trabajan tus padres?	*What do your parents do?*
Mi madre/padre es (comerciante).	*My mother/father is (a shop-owner).*

albañil, abogado/a	*bricklayer, lawyer*	jubilado/a	*retired*
camarero/a, cartero/a	*waiter, post-person*	mecánico/a, médico/a	*mechanic, doctor*
comerciante, dentista	*shop-owner, dentist*	peluquero/a	*hairdresser*
empleado/a de	*employee of*	profesor/a	*teacher*
enfermero/a	*nurse*	programador/a	*programmer*
fotógrafo/a	*photographer*	recepcionista	*receptionist*
granjero/a	*farmer*	secretario/a	*secretary*
ingeniero/a	*engineer*	técnico/a	*technician*

el comercio	*business, commerce*	en el extranjero	*abroad*
un empleo	*a job*	buscar, hacer	*to look for, to do/make*
una empresa	*a firm, company*	estudiar, viajar	*to study, to travel*
la enseñanza	*teaching*	ganar dinero	*to earn money*
la hostelería	*hotel trade*	pedir una beca	*to ask for a grant*
los servicios médicos	*medical services*	obtener un préstamo	*to get a loan*
el turismo	*tourism*	casarse	*to get married*

Grammar

C Stem/radical-changing verbs

Some verbs have changes in the stem. This is the part which is left when the infinitive ending **–ar/-er/-ir** is removed. The endings are as normal.

	o/u – ue **poder** *(to be able to)*	e – ie **preferir** *(to prefer)*	e – i **pedir** *(to ask for/order)*
yo	p**ue**do	pref**ie**ro	p**i**do
tú	p**ue**des	pref**ie**res	p**i**des
él, ella, usted	p**ue**de	pref**ie**re	p**i**de
nosotros/as	podemos	preferimos	pedimos
vosotros/as	podéis	preferís	pedís
ellos, ellas, ustedes	p**ue**den	pref**ie**ren	p**i**den

Common verbs with changes **o/u – ue**

almorzar	*to have lunch*	encontrar	*to find, to meet*
aprobar	*to pass (exam)*	jugar, morir	*to play, to die*
costar, doler	*to cost, to hurt*	soler	*to be used to*
dormir	*to sleep*	volver	*to return*

Common verbs with changes **e – ie**

cerrar, empezar	*to close, to begin*	pensar, perder	*to think, to lose*
entender	*to understand*	querer	*to want to, to love*
fregar	*to wash up*	recomendar	*to recommend*
merendar	*to have a snack*	sentir	*to feel, to be sorry*
nevar, helar	*to snow, to freeze*	tener*, venir*	*to have, to come*

*(yo) tengo, (yo) vengo

Common verbs with changes **e – i**

competir	*to compete*	repetir, seguir	*to repeat, to follow*
conseguir	*to succeed*	servir	*to serve*
corregir, elegir	*to correct, to choose*	vestir(se)	*to get dressed*

D Comparatives

To compare things, use the following:

más ... que	more than	Ella es más alta que yo. *She is taller than me.*
menos ... que	less than fewer than	Hay menos chicos que chicas. *There are fewer boys than girls.*
tan ... como	as ... as ...	Soy tan inteligente como tú. *I am as intelligent as you.*

Note irregulars: **mejor** *(better)*, **peor** *(worse)*, **mayor** *(older)*, **menor** *(younger)*.

Work experience

Talk and write about your work experience.

This topic provides a good opportunity for using a range of tenses.

A Work experience

READ

As part of the assessments in writing and speaking, you may be able to use your work experience as a topic: **las prácticas de laborales**.

Start off by matching the questions 1–8 below with their Spanish equivalents a–h in the conversation at the bottom of the page.

Ejemplo: 1 e

1 What were your hours like?

2 How did you get to work?

3 When was the lunch break?

4 Where did you do your work experience?

5 Were there any breaks?

6 How long did it take to get there?

7 Did you like the work?

8 How long did your work experience last?

B Giving details

SPEAK

Even if the work was repetitive (**repetitivo**) or your boss was a pain (**mi jefe/a era pesado/a**), your work mates were probably nice (**mis compañeros eran simpáticos**)!

Practica la conversación siguiente. Inventa otra y utiliza los apuntes en inglés. *Practise the following conversation. Invent another one using the notes in English.*

a *¿Dónde hiciste tus practicas laborales?* – Trabajé en un laboratorio.

b *¿Cuánto tiempo duraron?* – Duraron quince días.

c *¿Cómo ibas a tu trabajo?* – Iba en metro.

d *¿Cuánto tiempo tardabas en llegar?* – Tardaba unos treinta minutos.

e *¿Cómo era tu horario?* – Trabajaba de ocho a cuatro.

f *¿Había descansos?* – Sí. Había dos descansos de quince minutos.

g *¿Cuándo era la hora de comer?* – Era de doce a una.

h *¿Te gustaba el trabajo?* – Sí. En general era bastante interesante, pero a veces era aburrido.

> **exam tip >>**
>
> Try and use some of the following expressions to add colour and variety to what you say: *si te digo la verdad* (to tell the truth), *francamente* (frankly), *en realidad* (in fact), *en general* (on the whole) *or a veces/ de vez en cuando* (sometimes).

Work experience: 10 days in travel agents. Went by bus and on foot – took nearly an hour! Hours: 9–5.30, with lunch from 1–2. Breaks: 3 x 20 mins. Great fun on the whole, but a bit repetitive sometimes.

C Preparing for the speaking assessment

WRITE

1 As part of the speaking assessments, you may be able to talk about your work exprience.

2 The world of work can be a good topic to choose, because you can use a range of tenses.

3 To prepare for your assessment, make written notes on the following topic headings. Where it says (infin.) you will need to use an infinitive, for example, **suelo trabajar** *(I usually work)*.

> **remember >>**
>
> **You can't read from your notes when giving a presentation, but you are allowed several postcard-sized pieces of paper with a few headings in Spanish on each one to prompt you.**

Present tense
- trabajo – *I work*
- empiezo – *I start*
- termino – *I finish*
- gano – *I earn*
- me gusta – *I like*
- suelo (infin.) – *I usually*

Past tense
- trabajé – *I worked*
- fui allí – *I went there*
- empezaba – *I started*
- terminaba – *I finished*
- tenía que (infin.) – *I had to*
- me gustaba – *I liked*

Future tense
- voy a (infin.) – *I'm going to*
- tengo la intención de (infin.) – *I plan to*
- quisiera (infin.) – *I'd like to*
- iré – *I will go*
- espero (infin.) – *I hope to*
- pienso (infin.) – *I'm thinking of*

> **exam tip >>**
>
> **Check with your teacher how many words you can have on your prompt page, and whether you are allowed verbs in different tenses, or only in the infinitive form. Use a range of tenses to be eligible for higher marks.**

>> practice questions

Answer these questions in Spanish.

1 **¿Dónde trabajó Manolo el año pasado?**

2 **¿Qué opina de su empleo actual?**

3 **¿Qué le gustó más de su experiencia laboral?**

4 **¿Qué va a hacer después de los exámenes?**

5 **¿Cuál es la ventaja de trabajar en la frutería?**

6 **¿Qué país espera visitar?**

¡Hola! Me llamo Manolo. De lunes a viernes, trabajo en una frutería cerca de casa. Es aburrido, pero gano bastante. El otoño pasado hice mis prácticas laborales en una oficina de información y turismo, y me divertí mucho. Tenía que tratar con el público, lo que me gustaba mucho, pero preparar folletos turísticos en el ordenador era todavía mejor. Después de los exámenes hay posibilidad de trabajar en la misma oficina, pero quiero seguir estudiando el año próximo. También quisiera viajar al extranjero – el año pasado fui a México con mi familia, y tal vez un día iré a vivir a otro país sudamericano como Bolivia.

CVs and applying for a job

- Getting to know about official forms, such as ID forms or a CV feature fairly frequently in the exam.

- You need to understand job advertisements.

A Your CV

WRITE

1. In the exam, you may be asked to show you understand a CV or you may include one as part of a writing assessment.

2. The headings on this CV will also be useful for simpler forms or ID cards.

   Rellena el formulario con los detalles de abajo. *Complete the form with the details below.*

CURRÍCULUM VÍTAE

1	Apellidos:	....
2	Nombre:	....
3	Edad:	....
4	Fecha de nacimiento:	....
5	Lugar de nacimiento:	....
6	Nacionalidad:	....
7	Estado Civil:	....
8	D.N.I./Pasaporte:	....
9	Dirección (+código postal):	....
10	Teléfono:	....
11	Estudios:	....
12	Experiencia profesional:	....
13	Información complementaria: (p.ej. pasatiempos)	....
14	Empleo ideal:	....

remember >>

Spanish forms ask for surnames (*apellidos*) because Spaniards have two names: the father's and the mother's surname.

García Morales	Carmen	17 años	10-4-1984
Calle San Agustín, 18, 2ºD, 28002, Madrid	Médica	Lima, Perú	Peruana
Fotografía/baloncesto	Soltera	Instituto San Ignacio, Madrid (ESO, Bachillerato)	
(91) 746 65 71	Prácticas de laborales en el Hospital San Juan de Dios		36 741 802C

B Job advertisements

In the next activity, you'll be reading four short job advertisements and matching each job to the most appropriate person.

First scan the texts which you have to match up. Can you see any similarities between any of the words in the speech bubbles and the words in the advertisements? For example, **hermanas** might be connected to **hijos**. What other connections can you find?

remember >>

Don't worry if you can't understand every word.

Para cada joven, busca el anuncio más apropiado.
Find the most appropriate advertisement for each young person.

Begoña [ ]

David [ ]

Juanjo [ ]

Begoña
Me gustaría trabajar en el sector del turismo o de la hostelería durante el verano. El año pasado, pasé tres meses trabajando como ayudante general en la recepción del hostal de mi tía.

David
Entre semana, de cinco de la tarde a nueve, trabajo en la tienda del polideportivo o en el gimnasio. El verano que viene, quisiera buscar un empleo que pueda hacer los sábados y domingos solamente.

Juanjo
Soy el mayor, y tengo que cuidar a mis dos hermanas de cuatro y siete años después de las clases, el sábado ¡también! El año pasado, trabajé como monitor en la guardería de un hotel.

1
Buscamos:
chico/a para ayudar a padres con dos hijos (2 y 6) durante los meses de verano. Experiencia deseable.
Tel. (91) 592 61 44

2
Deporte Joven:
chico/a para fines de semana. Ayudar en almacén. Buena voluntad más importante que experiencia.
Tel. (91) 296 23 59

3
Se busca: personal para temporada julio–septiembre.
Hotel-Residencia El Almirante.
Camareros/as, recepcionistas, limpieza. Tel: (91) 238 91 61

>> practice questions

Invent a speech bubble for Ramón, who is interested in this post. He has no experience of camping but has worked in the Tourist Office.

¿Le interesa pasar el verano en la playa?
Buscamos jóvenes con experiencia para camping Costa Verde: montar tiendas y ayudar en la oficina de información.
Interesados llamar: (91) 380 43 29.

exam tip >>

Look for opportunities in speaking and writing to use a range of tenses.

Future work

 Say what your plans for the future are.

 Prepare an exended piece of writing, using a variety of tenses.

A Future plans

WRITE

You need to prepare a short paragraph about your hopes and plans for the future. Use the language in the boxes A–C to help.

First, work out how to say the sentences 1–6 in Spanish.

Escribe las frases 1–6 en español. *Write sentences 1–6 in Spanish.*

A

voy a
quiero
quisiera
me gustaría

B

buscar
ir
hacer
estudiar
seguir
trabajar
tener
tratar
viajar

C

a la universidad
estudiando en el colegio
en el sector de la industria
en los servicios médicos
en el sector del turismo
en el comercio
en la enseñanza
un empleo manual/físico
un empleo artístico/académico

con niños (pequeños)
con el público
con los animales
en equipo
en la investigación
mi propia empresa
al extranjero
en la ingenería
en la hostelería

This is a good topic in which to use a variety of tenses to impress the examiner!

For the pure future, take any of the infinitives from box B above, and add **-é**. For example: **Buscaré un empleo artístico.** (*I will look for an artistic job.*)

For the conditional, add **-ía** to the infinitive. For example: **Si tuviera dinero, viajaría mucho.** (*If I had money, I would travel a lot.*) Look back at page 70 if you need more help.

study hint >>

You can bring language from other topics in here: you might like to say what you're good at at school, to explain what you want to do in the future, e.g. *Se me dan muy bien las ciencias y saco muy buenas notas. Por eso (for this reason), me gustaría trabajar en la investigación.*

1 I want to work in teaching, with small children.

2 I'm going to carry on studying at school.

3 I'd like to look for a manual job.

4 I'd like to have my own business.

5 I want to travel abroad.

6 I'd like to work in a team, in the medical services.

84

B Job applications

You may be asked to read a longer passage or letter. You may have to give this information in the speaking or writing assessment. It needs to include a range of tenses, descriptions and opinions.

Read the letter below, and do the activity.

>> **key fact** To be eligible for higher marks, use a variety of tenses.

Escoge la palabra correcta para cada espacio. *Choose the correct word for each gap.*

a chicas

b asignaturas

c útil

d puestos

e cuatro

f niños

g bastante

h trabajar

i desorganizada

j fácil

k verano

l trabajadora

> **remember >>**
>
> **If you're aiming at a grade C or above, you need to show how you can use a variety of tenses: a past tense, the present tense and a future tense.**

62 Barnham Way,
Glasgow,
Escocia,
16 de marzo

Muy señor mío:
Acabo de ver su ofertando plazas vacantes para ...(1)... monitores en el camping Arenas Doradas en su página de web, y quisiera solicitar uno de estos ...(2)... .

Me gustaría trabajar en España durante el ...(3)... que viene, para mejorar mis conocimientos de la lengua española. El español es una de las ocho ...(4)... que estudio para hacer los exámenes de GCSE (equivalente a la ESO en España) en junio. Lo entiendo muy bien y lo hablo ...(5)... bien. También sé hablar un poco de francés, lo que será muy ...(6)... en un camping cerca de la frontera con Francia.

El año pasado, trabajé como monitora en un hotel en el oeste de Escocia. Me gustó mucho. Me llevé muy bien con los ...(7)..., y soy muy educada, reponsable y ...(8)... Estaré disponible para ...(9)... a mediados de julio y puedo seguir trabajando hasta finales de septiembre.

Quedo a la espera de sus gratas noticias.
Le saluda atentamente,

Janice Armstrong

>> practice questions

Write a letter in Spanish to the Hotel Espléndido, requesting the post which most appeals to you. Use Janice's letter as a model.

Hotel Espléndido, Paseo Marítimo, MÁLAGA: buscamos camareros/as y ayudantes (piscina, guardería), verano julio–septiembre.

> **exam tip >>**
>
> **Check over your writing in the exam. Pay attention to nouns and the endings of adjectives (masculine/feminine, and singular/plural), and verbs (correct tense and person).**

Social concerns

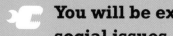

> ● **You will be expected to understand information about social issues.**

> ● **You may have to answer questions about attitudes and feelings.**

A Concerns for the future

>> **key fact** Look for the overall theme in each piece of text.

READ

① Read each text and match them to one of the topics A–F.

Escribe cada número 1–4 en la casilla apropiada. *Write each number 1–4 in the correct box.*

1 Lo que más me preocupa, es el futuro: el horror del desempleo. Mi padre, como muchos otros, pasó diez años sin ganar dinero, y yo no quiero ser como él. Mi pueblo antes estaba lleno de vida, pero ahora está muerto.
Ángel

2 Lo más difícil para mí, es que todos mis compañeros se emborrachan y se drogan regularmente. Hasta este momento, he resistido – ¿pero en el futuro ...?
Carmelina

3 Mis padres esperan que yo vaya a seguir los pasos de mi abuelo y mi hermano mayor, y sea médico – pero no quiero. No me interesa. Preferiría viajar un poco, ver el mundo. No estoy bastante seguro de mí mismo para decírselo.
Íñigo

4 Aunque yo nací aquí, y tengo pasaporte de este país, no me trata bien la gente. Los que somes de otro color – es decir, no somos blanco es – tenemos que aguantar la discriminación y los insultos en la calle. A veces, me hace llorar.
Zohora

A	la guerra		D	las expectativas de la familia	
B	el racismo		E	la presión de los amigos	
C	el paro		F	el hambre	

② Although young people speak about their present concerns, they have used several tenses. Read their thoughts again and find examples of the following tenses:

Ángel: preterite, imperfect

Carmelina: perfect

Íñigo: conditional

Zohora: preterite

B Reading between the lines

>> **key fact** **You will need to identify attitudes and emotions.**

READ

You will be expected to listen for people's moods and how they are feeling.

Re-read the four texts from A, and answer the questions in English.

1 Why does Ángel not want to follow in his father's footsteps?

2 What is Ángel's village like now?

3 What would Íñigo prefer to do?

4 Why does Íñigo find it difficult to talk to his family?

5 How does Zohora feel about what happens to her in the street?

6 How would you describe Carmelina's attitude to the future?

> **exam tip >>**
>
> **Check the number of marks allocated to each question. If it says 'two marks' then you need to give two pieces of information.**

C Your thoughts

>> **key fact** **You can use simple language to talk about complex issues.**

WRITE

- You may be asked, as part of a speaking or writing assessment, to talk about your anxieties for the future: e.g.

  1 ¿Cuáles son los problemas sociales más importantes?

  2 ¿Cuáles son las cosas que más te preocupan?

- You can use a verb + noun combination: '**Es**' (for one thing) or '**Son**' for more than one. E.g.

  – **Es el hambre.** *(It's hunger).*

  – **Son la violencia y la guerra.** *(It's violence and war)*

- Beginning with a verb of feeling/emotion is another possibility: look back at page 3.

  Me irrita la nueva cultura de los famosos – no es sana.
  (I'm irritated by the new celebrity culture – it's not healthy.)

- Look back at the following topics for additional language to help:

Relationships	pp. 3, 11	New technologies	pp. 12, 20–21	Media	pp. 51, 52–53
Health-related issues	pp. 12, 16–17	The environment	pp. 36, 42–43		

>> practice questions

WRITE

Choose one of the two questions above and write your reply: aim for 3–4 lines if you can, and more if you wish. Use the page references above to help.

Listening section D

You will need to use the CD-ROM to complete this section.

A School

Listen to Juan and Rosario talking about their schools. Who mentions which topics? Put a ✔ in the appropriate boxes in the grid.

Look at the words in the grid: which Spanish words might you expect to hear?

exam tip >>

Listen for gist here: the overall themes. You can ignore the details.

	Size	Type	Number of pupils	Ages of pupils	Buildings
Juan					
Rosario					

B Uniform

1 Juan talks about his uniform. Complete the grid in English.

	Item	Colour
A	....	black
B	jumper	....
C	....	white
D	tie	black, ..., grey

study hint >>

Knowing your grammar will help here. The colour adjective comes after the noun in Spanish, e.g. *una bolsa marrón* (a brown bag).

2 Listen again. Complete the two gaps in English.

Juan thinks his uniform is:

A ....   B ....

C Facilities

Where are the classrooms situated? Write the correct letter for each subject in the appropriate box.

A German
B English
C Art

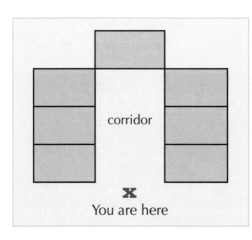

corridor

X
You are here

study hint >>

Make sure you know the words for first, second, third etc. They are used in lots of different topics.

D Subjects

>> **key fact** Negative expressions do not always contain 'no': *nunca/jamás* (never) and *tampoco* (neither) may come at the start of a sentence.

1 Maite talks about her school subjects. Put a tick ✔ if she likes a subject, and a cross (✘) if she does not like it.

A

B

C

D

2 Listen again. Write in English her reason for liking/disliking each of these subjects.

A Geography ....

B Maths ....

E Jobs

>> **key fact** The exam will test your knowledge of verb tenses; past, present, future/conditional.

Pablo is talking about his parents' jobs. Write your answers in the grid: you will need to complete only four (4) of them.

	Used to work in	Now works in/as	Would not like to work in
Father			
Mother			

F Work and Future Plans

>> **key fact** Listening tasks at Higher Level are longer and more complex. Get as much listening practice as you can.

Listen to the conversation between Cristina and Paco. Answer the sentences in English.

1 What does Cristina ask Paco?

2 What is Paco going to start?

3 What is Cristina no longer doing?

4 What does she want to do in the future? Mention two (2) things.

5 What was Ignacio's previous part-time job?

6 Why was he good at it?

7 Why is he doing his current job? Give two (2) reasons.

study hint >>

Learn phrases which indicate time frames: *todavía* (still), *ya ... no* (not now), *de momento* (at the moment), *en el futuro* (in the future), *ahora* (now), *antes* (before)

Exam questions and model answers

![Listening]

Listening

There are many different task types in the exam. You will have met a number of them already in the listening tasks at the end of each section. Here are further examples with some for you to try for yourself on the opposite page.

You will need the CD-ROM to complete this section.

>> Tasks with grids

Do not panic if the grid seems to contain a lot of information.

There will be one topic not mentioned, so one column will not have a tick in it.

Put a ruler or a piece of paper horizontally across the grid and move it down as you complete it.

This will help you focus and make sure you do not put a cross in the incorrect row.

In this type of task, you do not have to focus on specific details, so ignore them!

Example 1

Read the following list. What are they talking about? Put ✗ in the correct box.

	Sport	Shopping	Reading	TV	Computers	Cinema
1				✗		
2	✗					
3						✗
4		✗				
5					✗	

Tip As you look at the English prompts, think about the Spanish words you may hear.

>> Choosing the correct words

You may have to chose a word from a list to complete a sentence or fill a gap.

Check the instructions: you may not have to write the word in full, but simply the number or letter beside it.

Read the list of words first. It will take less time than reading the rest of the task, and they will already give you clues as to the content. E.g. 'waitress' and 'shop assistant' lets you know you need to listen for types of jobs.

Now read the rest of the task: any clues as to which words (e.g. places, jobs, times) might be appropriate in each gap?

Example 2

LIsten to Luisa talking about her work. Read the list of words and the sentences.

For each sentence write the correct letter in the box.

A	sore feet	**D**	Saturday	**G**	kind	**J**	a headache
B	busy	**E**	4-10	**H**	home	**K**	shop assistant
C	school	**F**	waitress	**I**	10-4	**L**	Sunday

1 She works as a **F**
2 She works near her **H**
3 Her day of work is **D**

4 Work hours are **I**
5 By the end of the day, she has **A**
6 The people are very **G**

Tip Each time you choose a word, cross it off the list. It will make it easier for you to see what is left.

>> Some questions for you to try

Question 1

Read the following list. Which aspects of holidays are they talking about? Put ✗ in the correct box.

5 marks

	future plans	usual holiday	opinion	activities	weather	means of travel
1						
2						
3						
4						
5						

Extra practice

Listen again to the last item (number 5) and answer the questions.

1 Who are the holiday companions?   **2** How long is the holiday?

Question 2

LIsten to Eduardo talking about his school. Read the list of words and the sentences.

For each sentence write the correct letter in the box.

A boring   **D** sweets   **G** chewing gum   **J** secondary
B uniform   **E** public   **H** unnecessary   **K** what they like
C clear   **F** necessary   **I** strict   **L** stupid

1 The rules are very ☐   **4** You can't eat ☐
2 He thinks they are ☐   **5** He is at a ☐ school.
3 Some of them are ☐   **6** Pupils wear ☐

Question 3

Enrique talks about his experience of places to live and visit.

Tick the correct box for each place 1–5.

		Past	Present	Future
1	outskirts city			
2	small village			
3	grandparents home			
4	mountains			
5	coast			

Speaking Assessments

>> Gearing yourself up

There are a variety of possible speaking assessments on a wide range of topics, so check with your teacher what the requirements of your exam board are:

- How many assessments (usually two) and when will they be?

- Which topics will they cover, and which aspect of that topic? You may have some choice in deciding this.

- What kind of speaking tasks are they? They usually have to be of different types, lasting 4-6 minutes. Common task types are:

  - an open interaction, like a conversation

  - an unscripted role-play task, with unexpected elements

  - a free-flowing discussion based on a visual like a picture, photo or small object

  - a short presentation (2-3 minutes) with a discussion afterwards

  - a pair-work or group task, in which you will need to ensure that your contribution allows you to perform to the maximum of your ability.

>> Sharpening your focus

In the full GCSE course, the speaking assessment counts for 30% of the total marks for the exam, so it is worth preparing carefully.

Regular classwork and homework needs to part of your preparation. Effort put in during the year will pay off. Learn new vocabulary regularly, give yourself extra practice using the Bitesize book and website, and keep your files and vocabulary books/files well-organised. Take them with you to the supervised preparation session.

>> Fine-tuning your preparation

- Check what you will be able to take into the assessment: usually the task sheet, and your notes and a visual stimulus if wished.

- Let's look at how to make best use of the 30 or 40 words (check your exam board requirements) which you are allowed to take in with you.

The task sheet tells you what to prepare:		You need to aim for:
a how people describe you	→	Content: plenty of detail
b good friend/someone you admire	→	Express ideas/views
c things that annoy you about family/friends	→	Range of tenses
d which relationships are important to you and why	→	Show initiative: ask questions
e difficulties/pressures in relationships	→	Speak confidently and clearly
You will also be expected to respond to two items you have not prepared.	→	Cope with unpredictable. Think ahead – what might be asked?

Your notes may contain up to five bullet points, and 6 or 8 Spanish words per point; Some boards allow you to have conjugated verbs (ie. already in tense form), others require verbs in their infinitive form only. Check with your teacher.

Here are Sally's notes. Look at her choice of words and read her reasons for them below.

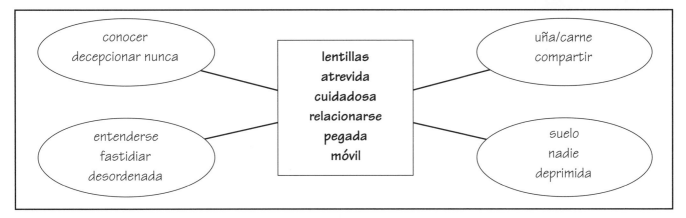

Here are Sally's thoughts on how she planned to use her notes, with comments on how well she completed the task.

Sally: Going to describe self physically, hate glasses, got contact lenses (**lentillas**), my character (**atrevida**, **cuidadosa**), get on well with people (**relacionarse**), love communicating, glued (**pegada**) to my mobile (**móvil**).

Comment: plenty of detail, expresses likes and dislikes, good vocabulary.

Sally: Best friend, got to know (**conocer**) her first day primary school, never (**nunca**) lets me down (**decepcionar**), joined at hip (**como uña y carne**), will share (**compartir**) flat one day.

Comment: Excellent and natural use of tense here. Preterite (**la conocí** – I got to know her), and future (**compartiremos un piso**). Evidence of independent research to find appropriate colloquial expression for 'joined at the hip'.

Sally: Don't get on well (**entenderse**) with my sister, have to share (got '**compartir**' already) room, she really annoys (**fastidiar**) me at times, very messy (**desordenada**). Last weekend, left (**dejar**) her stuff all over the floor (**suelo**), she doesn't respect ('**respetar**' same as English easy to remember) anyone (**no … nadie** + not … anyone). Also lazy – I don't know what she will do with her life. Sometimes I feel really depressed. But I do love her!

Comment: fulfils task amply, good use of vocabulary for feelings and emotions. Another use of past tense (**dejó todas sus cosas en el suelo**) and future (**no sé lo que hará en su vida**).

Here are some tips for making the most of your notes in the Speaking Assessment, like Sally.

- Be selective. Don't write down vocabulary you already find it easy to remember, especially if it's similar to English. Write down items you find harder to remember, or words which will remind you what to say next in the topic.
- Think 'variety of tenses'. Where can you do this: is there somewhere in each bullet point where it would be natural to use another tense? Don't save them all for the last minute or two of the assessment.
- Use vocabulary you know well, and are comfortable with – do not look up lots of unfamilar expressions at the last moment, because you will not remember or use them with ease, and your speaking will not flow well.

Over to you!

Prepare your own notes, using the task sheet on the facing page.

What can your learn from Sally about preparing well?

Use your notes by practicing speaking aloud in front of a mirror. Learn how to glance at them while still speaking, so you can keep going smoothly.

Work with a friend, and exchanges helpful comments.

¡Buena suerte!

>> Reading tasks with pictures

This is one of the simpler task types in the exam. You need to choose the sentence which matches each picture best. Be careful of 'false friends': words in Spanish which look like English ones, but mean something different.

Example 1

Leisure time activities. Write the correct number in each box.

A Cuando llueve, juego al ping-pong con mi hermana. `6`

B Si hace buen tiempo, me gusta andar en bici. `2`

C Me encanta nadar en el mar, si hace bastante calor. `4`

D A veces, vamos de excursión en autocar a la sierra. `1`

1	2	3	4	5	6

>> Drawing conclusions

This type of task is more challenging. You have to decide what the writers think or feel.

The text may not give the information directly – you will have to read between the lines.

Be careful with negatives. Do not assume that this means the writer feels negative!

Example 2

Three young people write about their area. Put a tick ✔ in the correct box.

P = Positive. N = Negative. I = Indifferent/doesn't care.

1 Las calles están sucias, hay ventanas rotas, papeles por todas partes y no hay ningún sitio donde pueden jugar los niños.

2 No paso mucho tiempo en mi barrio, y no me doy cuenta de como es. Tengo una novia en las afueras, y suelo ir allí los fines de semana. Me da igual.

3 Aunque las calles están estrechas y la gente no tiene mucho dinero, mi barrio está muy animada. Todo el mundo es simpático y no hay ni violencia ni jaleo.

	P	N	I
1		✔	
2			✔
3	✔		

>> Some similar questions for you to try

Question 1

Free time activities. Write the correct letter in the box.

1	En mi tiempo libre me gusta mucho leer.	
2	Me encantan las películas de aventura.	
3	Cuando puedo, voy de paseo en el campo.	
4	¿Lo que más me gusta? ¡Tomar el sol en la playa!	

 a c e

 b d f

Question 2

Young people give their view on their holidays. Tick the correct box.

P = Positive. N = Negative. P+N = Positive and Negative.

1 El hotel era muy cómodo, y muy cerca de la playa. Lo peor era el ruido: había una discoteca cerca, donde bailaban hasta las tres de la madrugada.

2 ¡Hacer camping cuando llueve todos los días no es agradable! Ropa mojada, agua en los cereales, frío por la noche – ¡no ha sido la mejor experiencia de mi vida!

3 Pasamos una en un barco de vela, con seis otras personas que no conocimos antes. ¡Ahora, sí! Hicimos viajes bonitos por la costa, pero no había mucho sitio.

	P	N	P+N
1			
2			
3			

Question 3

What's the weather like in each area? Write the correct letter on the dotted line.

A Castilla y León: continuarán hoy las temperaturas muy bajas, sobre todo en la meseta.

B Cantábrico: lluvias intensas y chubascos por la mañana. Sin cambio en la temperaturas.

C Andalucía: las temperaturas llegarán hasta los 35 grados esta tarde. Vientos flojos del oeste.

D Islas Baleares: neblinas matinales, cielo despejado por la tarde.

E Cataluña: aumento de nubosidad por la tarde en toda la zona. Ligero descenso de temperaturas, que alcanzarán los veintidós grados.

F Islas Canarias: sin cambio en las temperaturas por la mañana, con vientos fuertes del componente oeste. Más tarde, riesgo de lluvias débiles.

1 Cielo nublado en ...

....

2 Hará mucho viento en ...

....

3 Hará frío en ...

....

4 Lloverá mucho en ...

....

5 Hará muchísimo calor en ...

....

>> Finding out about the task

- As with the Speaking Assessments, there are a wide variety of ways in which you will be able to show the full range of your writing ability: posters, blogs, emails, postcards, applications for work, letters of complaint, and accounts of your interests, daily life, issues which affect you, hopes and anxieties about the future. Check with your teacher what your particular exam board offers.

- A common format is a task with bullet points as prompts. Note whether it says you **must** cover them or whether you **could** include them. The latter offers you more flexibility and lets you use your imagination and creativity.

- Many of the Practice activities in Bitesize have been designed to give you the opportunity to tackle mini-tasks in this way. (E.g. pp. 7, 11, 15, 17, 19, 41, 53, 55, 61, 65, 87). Speaking tasks help increase your language skills.

- You will be expected to write your final piece within a given time, and in supervised conditions. Before that, there will be a period of preparation possibly over several weeks, in which you know what the task is and will be able to use that time to prepare. You will be able to take some notes in Spanish into with you: ask your teacher how many words you are allowed (usually bweeen 30-40).

>> Knowing what to aim for

Since the writing assessment in the full GCSE accounts for 30% of the marks, it is worth allocating extra time to improve your writing. Any increase in vocabulary, grammar and skills of expression will also help your speaking ability. Here are some of the things which examiners are looking for at the higher grades:

- plenty of information and detail, ability to describe and narrate events

- ability to express opinion or views and justify them, giving reasons

- use of sequencing, and different time frames

>> Upping your grade

These activities will help you understand more clearly how to improve your writing and give you practice.

1 Describing people, places and events.

Adjectives enrich your writing, adding colour and detail. Compare the following.

> Cené en un restaurante en el campo.

> Cené en un restaurante muy típico y cómodo, situado en un paisaje tranquilo con vistas maravillosas hacia la sierra cubierta de nieve.

> The word 'y' (and) becomes 'e' before a word which starts with an 'i/hi' e.g. *chicos españoles e ingleses.*

Q How many adjectives does the second sentence use? What is the usual position of an adjective in relation to the noun? What joins adjectives together?

Your turn! Rewrite this sentence making it as descriptive as you can using as many of the words in brackets as you can. Don't forget that adjectives have to agree with the noun. (p.9).

> Visité un pueblo al pie de la montaña.

antiguo, interesante, enclavado (nestling), bonito, verde, estupendo, nube (cloud) **blanco.**

2 Expressing your opinion

Give your opinion extra emphasis: compare the two views below.

En mi opinión, el teléfono móvil es útil.

Personalmente, el teléfono móvil me parece imprescindible, hoy en día. Por un lado los móviles son útiles, pero por otro una verdadera molestia. (*nuisance*)

Other ways of saying 'I think': *a mi parecer, creo*. For explaining the views of others, you can use *según* (according to). E.g. *según mi padre* (according to my Dad)

Q What's the Spanish for: speaking personally, I think (it seems to me), on the one hand, on the other?

Your turn! Rewrite this viewpoint using phrases which highlight your opinion and contrast it with a different point of view.

En mi opinion, el iPod es estúpido.

a mi modo de ver, me parece, divertido, por una parte, entretenido, por otra, un artículo de lujo (luxury).

3 Sequencing

This means giving using words like 'and then', 'later', after' so that your narrative of an event flows well. Compare these two accounts:

Llegamos al aeropuerto. Había un problema con el avión. Llegamos al hotel tarde.

Primero, llegamos al aeropuerto a tiempo. Pero luego - despúes de pasar tres horas en las cafeterías y tiendas – nos dijeron (*they told us*) que había un problema con el avión. Seis horas más tarde, aterrizamos en Málaga finalmente.

You can use *después* (after/wards) on its own, or *después de* + infinitive. E.g. *después de comer* (after eating).

Q How many time related (first, then etc.) expressions can you find?

Your turn! Rewrite this account, using sequences words and phrases.

Llegamos al concierto de pop. Hubo un problema con las entradas (*tickets*). Entramos en el estadio.

En primer lugar, luego, pasar tres horas en una cola (queue), **las entradas** (tickets), **dos horas más tarde, entramos en el estadio, por fin.**

Also useful are: *a tiempo* (on time), *al principio* (at the start), *al final* (at the end), *mientras tanto* (meanwhile).

As you revise, continue to extend and enrich your writing using these three tips.

¡Buena suerte!

Complete the grammar

A, some (p. 4)

Fill in the gaps.

	masculine	feminine
(s)	<u>un</u> hermano *a brother*	__ hermana *a sister*
(pl)	__ hombres *some men*	__ mujeres *some women*

The (p. 4)

Fill in the gaps.

	masculine	feminine
(s)	<u>el</u> tío *the uncle*	__ tía *the aunt*
(pl)	__ chicos *the boys*	__ chicas *the girls*

Plural nouns (p. 4)

Make the nouns plural.

un libro	30	___libros___
una mesa	15	_____
un tablón	4	_____
un ordenador	3	_____
una luz	8	_____
un estante	2	_____
un póster	5	_____

Adjectives (p. 4)

Write the feminine adjective.

masculine	feminine
italiano	**italiana**
catalán	
escocés	
español	
marrón	
rosa	

The present tense (p. 5)

Complete the verb endings.

	hablar *(to speak)*	comer *(to eat)*	vivir *(to live)*
yo	hablo	com__	viv__
tú	habl__	comes	viv__
él, ella, usted	habl__	come	vive
nosotros/as	hablamos	com__	vivimos
vosotros/as	habláis	coméis	viv__
ellos, ellas, ustedes	habl__	comen	viven

Irregular present tense verbs (p. 5)

a Write in the 'yo' form of each verb.

dar *(to give)*	*doy*	saber *(to know how to)*	
conocer *(to know a person)*		salir *(to go out, leave)*	
hacer *(to do, make)*		traer *(to bring)*	
poner *(to put, set, lay)*		ver *(to see)*	

Irregular present tense verbs (p. 5)

a Write in the 'yo' form of each verb.

IR	*(to go)*	voy			va		vais
TENER	*(to have)*		tienes			tenemos	tienen
ESTAR	*(to be)*			está		estáis	
SER	*(to be)*	soy				somos	

b Fill in the blanks.

There are two verbs *to be*: **ser**, **estar**.

Use [ ] to indicate position, and temporary moods.

Use [ ] for describing people, places, things.

c Complete the missing parts of the verbs.

The immediate future (p. 27)

Fill in the blanks.

To say what you're going to do:

Use the verb [ ] ,

followed by [*a*] , and the

[ ] of another verb.

Gustar (p. 13)

Fill in the gaps.

Me gust<u>a</u> el dibujo.
No me gust_ la historia.
Me gust_ _ las matemáticas.
No me gust_ _ los deberes.

Comparatives (p. 79)

Fill in the missing words.

more than	más _____
less than	_____ que
as ... as	tan ... _____

tanto ruido	*so much noise*
_____ polución	*so much pollution*
_____ coches	*so many cars*
_____ chicas	*so many girls*

Indirect object pronouns (p. 13)

Fill in the gaps.

I like	**me** gusta/n
you like	__ gusta/n
he/she likes, you like	__ gusta/n
we like	__ gusta/n
you like	**os** gusta/n
they/you like	__ gusta/n

Asking questions (p. 26)

Write in the Spanish.

where?	*¿dónde?*
how much?	_____
how?	_____
what?	_____
when?	_____
who?	_____
why?	_____

Positive commands (p. 27)

Fill in the missing endings or parts.

	TÚ	USTED
-ar	habl**a**	habl_
-er	com_	com_
-ir	escrib_	escrib_

	TÚ	USTED
(cruzar)	cruza	
(torcer)		tuerza
(coger)	coge	
(seguir)		siga

Reflexive verbs (p. 5)

Fill in the missing reflexive pronouns:

yo	___ lavo
tú	___ lavas
él, ella, usted	___ lava
nosotros/as	**nos** lavamos
vosotros/as	**os** laváis
ellos, ellas, ustedes	___ lavan

A/de (p. 26)

Fill in the blanks.

a The Spanish for *to* is **a**.

When followed by **el** it becomes

[_____] .

b The Spanish for *of* or *from* is **de**.

When followed by **el** it becomes

[_____] .

The perfect tense (p. 59)

Fill in the missing endings or parts.

	YO	
-ar (dejar)	he	dej _____
-er (comer)	he	com _____
-ir (salir)	he	sal _____

he	**escrito**	*I've written*
		I've done
		I've put on, set
		I've broken
		I've seen

The regular preterite tense (p. 48)

Complete the verb endings.

	hablar	comer	vivir
yo	habl__	comí	viv__
tú	habl__	com__	viviste
él, ella, usted	habl__	comió	viv__
nosotros/as	hablamos	com__	vivimos
vosotros/as	hablasteis	com__	vivisteis
ellos, ellas, ustedes	habl__	comieron	viv__

Irregular preterite verbs (p. 49)

Fill in the missing parts of the verbs.

SER, IR	to be, to go	fui		fue		fuisteis	
DAR	to give		diste		dimos		dieron

The pretérito grave (p. 48)

Complete the endings.

INFINITIVE		STEM
to be	estar	**estuv-**
to do, make	hacer	
to be able to	poder	
to put, set	poner	
to want to	querer	
to have	tener	
to come	venir	

yo	**-e**
tú	-_____
él, ella, usted	**-o**
nosotros/as	-_____
vosotros/as	**-isteis**
ellos, ellas, ustedes	-_____

Stem/radical changing verbs (p. 79)

Complete the gaps correctly.

These verbs have changes to their stem in the yo, tú, él, ella, usted and ustedes form.

o	changes to	ue	poder (to be able to)	yo _____	I am able to
u		___	jugar (to play)	tú _____	
e		___	preferir (to prefer)	él _____	
e		i	pedir (to ask for)	ellas _____	

Direct object pronouns (p. 49)

a Fill in the missing pronouns.

SINGULAR	
me	me
_____	you (informal)
_____, le	it, him
_____	it, her
le (m), la (f)	you (formal)

PLURAL	
_____	us
os	you (informal)
_____ (m), las (f)	them (objects)
les (m), _____ (f)	them (people)
les (m), las (f)	you (formal)

b Fill in the blanks.

Direct object pronouns usually come

[   ] the verb:

E.g. ¿El pantalón? Lo compro.

They can be added on to the

[   ] of an infinitive:

E.g. ¿La camisa? Sí, quiero comprarla.

Demonstrative adjectives (p. 49)

Fill in the missing words.

	(ms)	(fs)
this	este	_____
that	_____	esa
that (there)	aquel	_____

	(mpl)	(fpl)
these	_____	estas
those	esos	_____
those (there)	_____	aquellas

Demonstrative pronouns (p. 49)

Fill in the gap.

(this/that one, these/those ones)

are the same as the adjectives

above, but have an [   ]

on the first 'e':

Verbs of obligation (p. 71)

Complete with the correct verbs.

(have to, must)	_____
(ought to, should)	_____
(one has to)	_____

Se ... (p. 13)

Complete the boxes

Se	+		=	One ... They ...
		_____ (person singular of the verb)		People ... We ...

(comer)	(beber)	(escribir)
Se come	Se _____	Se _____

The regular imperfect tense (p. 71)

Complete the endings.

	HABLAR	COMER	VIVIR
yo	hablaba	beb____	vivía
tú	habl____	bebías	viv____
él, ella, usted	hablaba	beb____	vivía
nosotros/as	habl____	bebíamos	viv____
vosotros/as	hablábais	beb____	vivíais
ellos, ellas, ustedes	habl____	bebían	viv____

Irregular imperfect tense verbs (p. 71)

Fill in the missing parts.

IR	(to go)	iba	_____	_____	íbamos	_____	_____
SER	(to be)	_____	eras	_____	_____	érais	_____
VER	(to see)	veía	_____	veía	_____	veíais	_____

The gerund and continuous tenses (p. 59)

Complete the gaps.

	Remove	Add	Example		
-ar verbs	-ar		andar	→	
-er verbs		-iendo	comer	→	
-ir verbs			escribir	→	

Present continuous: use the present tense of the verb [_____] + gerund.

Imperfect continuous: use the [_____] tense of the verb estar + gerund.

Which tense? (pp. 26, 48, 49, 59, 71)

Write in which of the following tenses you need and complete the gaps in Spanish:
- the present, the preterite, the immediate future, the perfect or the imperfect.

I live in Marbella	present	_____ en Marbella.
I am a bit careless.		_____ un poco descuidado.
I was going to visit a friend.		_____ a visitar a una amiga.
I have lost my mobile.		_____ mi móvil.
I left it on the bus.		Lo _____ en el autobús.
I am going to ring the office.		____ __ _____ a la oficina.

The future and conditional tenses (p. 70)

Fill in the blanks and complete the verb endings.

1   The future tense indicates what [   ] happen.

2   The conditional indicates what [   ] happen.

3   The endings are the same for [**-ar**] [   ] and [   ] verbs.

	FUTURE	CONDITIONAL
yo	hablaré	hablar__
tú	hablar___	hablarías
él, ella, usted	hablará	hablar___
nosotros/as	hablar___	hablaríamos
vosotros/as	hablaréis	hablar___
ellos, ellas, ustedes	hablar___	hablarían

Irregular future/conditional stems (p. 70)

Complete the verbs.

	INFINITIVE	STEM
to do, make	hacer	har-_____
to be able to	poder	_____
to put, set	poner	_____
to want to	querer	_____
to have	tener	_____
to come	venir	_____

Ser/estar (p. 10)

Complete the grid.

SER	
1	Permanent characteristics
2	
3	Time

ESTAR	
1	
2	Feelings, moods
3	

Negative commands (p. 37)

Fill in the missing endings.

	TÚ	USTED
-ar	no hables	no habl__
-er	no com__	no com__
-ir	no escrib__	no escrib__

	VOSOTROS	USTEDES
-ar	no habléis	no habl__
-er	no com__	no com__
-ir	no escrib__	no escrib__

Impersonal verbs (p. 37)

Complete correctly.

to hurt	doler
to delight	
to be lacking	
to be necessary	
to interest	
to remain, be left over	
to be an excess of	

Me _duele_ la espalda.

Te _____ el deporte, ¿no?

Le _____ un cuchillo.

Nos _____ más dinero.

Os _____ mucho el tenis, creo.

Les _____ tres manzanas.

Me _____ vino.

Adverbs (p. 37)

Fill in the boxes and complete the grids.

To form adverbs, take the masculine form of the [   ].

Now make it [   ] and add -mente.

rápido	→	_____	+	-mente	→	_____
lento	→	_____	-	-mente	→	_____
fácil	→	_____		-mente	→	_____

well	
badly	
slowly	

There are two words for 'quickly':

[   ]

[   ]

Check your grammar in the exam.

- Gender of nouns: do I need **el**, ..., **los** or ... ? Should it be ..., **una**, **unos**, ...?
- The word for *to/at* is **a**; followed by **el**, it becomes ... .
- The word for *of/from* is **de**: followed by **el**, it becomes ... .
- Endings on adjectives: masculine, ... , singular, ...?
- Endings on verbs: is this the correct .... (preterite/present/future, etc.)?
- Impersonal verbs like **gustar** need an indirect object pronoun: should it be **me**, ..., **le**, ..., **os**, ...?
- Direct object pronouns: use ... /**le, la, los, las** for people, and **lo, la, ..., las** for things.

Vocabulary extra: how much do you know?

The following two pages contain language and expressions which are useful across all topics. You will have met them in different places in Bitesize. Check your replies in the Answers Section, pp. 113.

Write the correct Spanish or English word in the box.

Connectives	
además	
aparte de	
dado que	
es decir	
por un lado	
por otro	
sin duda	

Negatives	
	never
	neither ... nor
	nothing
	no-one
	no/none
	not ... but (rather)
	not ... either, neither

Greetings and exclamations	
¡Basta!	
	Welcome!
¡Buen viaje!	
	Good luck!
¡Claro!	
	Careful!
¡Enhorabuena!	
	Happy Easter!
¡Felices vacaciones!	
	Congratulations!
¡Felicitaciones!	
	Happy New Year!
¡Feliz cumpleaños!	
	Happy Christmas!
¡Feliz santo!	
	Watch out!
¡Olé!	
	Enjoy your meal!
¡Que lo pase(s) bien!	
	Yuck!
¡Qué bien!	
	How ...!
¡Qué horror!	
	What a disaster!
¡Qué lástima!	
	What a shame!

Common Verbs	
	to give
	to owe/must
	to be
	to be
	to make, do
	there is/are
	one has to
	to go
	to be able to
	to want, love
	to have
	to have to
	to happen
	to hear
	to put, set
	to take place
	to come
	to return
	to become
	to go off/away
	to go up
	to go down
	to turn on
	to turn off
	to think
	to prefer

Expressions with tener (to have) Fill in the boxes correctly.

	to be ... years old	tener hambre	
	to be hot	tener miedo	
	to be careful	tener razón	
	to be successful	tener sed	
	to be cold	tener sueño	
	to feel like	tener suerte	

Adverbs and connectives Fill in the boxes correctly.

por mucho tiempo			unfortunately
a menudo			immediately
a veces			especially
muchas veces			more
abajo / arriba			very
ahí			perhaps
aquí			really
aunque			recently
bastante			always
casi			still, yet
demasiado			already
deprisa			straightaway

Quantities Write in the correct Spanish.

	a bottle of		a jar of
	a box of		a tub of
	a dozen of		half of
	a kilo of		a quarter of
	half a kilo/litre of		a third of
	a tin of		double, twice
	a litre of		a little of
	a packet of		enough, sufficient
	a piece of		only
	a slice of		several

Expressions of time and connecting words Complete the gaps.

a _ _ _ _ _ _ de	from	_ _ _ _	yesterday
_ _ _ _ _ mismo	right now	_ _ _ _ _	since
al día _ _ _ _ _ _ _ _ _	the next day	más _ _ _ _ _	later
de _ _ _ en _ _ _ _ _ _	from time to time	_ _ _ _ _ _ _	after
_ _ _ _ ayer	the day before yesterday	_	or
_ _ _ _ _ _ mañana	the day after tomorrow	_ _ _ _	but
el _ _ _ de semana	at the weekend	_ _ _ _	so

Answers

Pages 4–5

B Plural nouns: cuatro dormitorios, dos terrazas, dos balcones, tres pasillos, dos garajes, cuatro televisores

C Adjectives: baja, mayor, alta, delgada, verdes, castaño, educado, callada, impaciente, habladora, menores, inteligentes, graciosos

E Verbs: 1 conoces, eres **2** vivo, haces **3** estamos, tiene **4** es, vais **5** sé, salimos

Page 7

C Family and friends: 1-C, **2**-G, **3**-A, **4**-F, **5**-E, **6**-D

Page 8

A Daily routine: A2: 1 A qué hora **3** Cómo **5** Cuánto **7** Cuántas **9** Cuándo **11** Dónde **13** Cuántas **15** A qué hora

A4: 1 Se levanta **2** Lleva **3** Va **4** Sale **5** Tarda **6** Empiezan **7** Hay **8** Las clases duran **9** hay recreos **10** Terminan **11** Come **12** Vuelve **13** Hace **14** Le gusta **15** Se acuesta a

Page 9

B Helping at home: to cut, to tidy/ to pick up, to clean, to wash, to prepare, to sweep, to pass (... over), to set/put, to help, to water, to clear, to take out, to make/do, to wash up

B2: 1 ayudar **2** hacer **3** recoger/ limpiar **4** sacar **5** preparar **6** barrer **7** pasar, **8** poner **9** quitar **10** lavar **11** fregar/lavar **12** hacer **13** lavar **14** regar **15** limpiar/ recoger **16** sacar **17** cortar

B3: 1 todos los días, **2** a veces, **3** entre semana, **4** por la mañana, **5** por la tarde, **6** los sábados por la mañana, **7** el fin de semana, **8** en verano

Page 10

A Personality, moods and feelings: A2: Puri: Soy, Estoy. Luis: está. Diego: soy. Miki: Estoy, soy. Alisa: está, está. Rafa: Estoy.

A3: 1 Rafa, **2** Diego, **3** Miki, **4** Luis, **5** Puri, **6** Alisa, **7** Puri, **8** Diego, **9** Miki

Page 11

B Future relationships: B2: Sí: Carlita, Gabriel. No: Tere. No sé: Miguel, Rosa, Andrés

B3: 1 Study, set up his own business. **2** He is not sure if same sex marriage is permitted in his country. **3** Any three of: church, guests, honeymoon, wedding dress. **4** Problems with violence and alcohol. **5** Go to university, travel abroad. **6** Any two of: she's not interested in wasting time looking after a husband, ruining her body with one pregnancy after another.

Page 13

E Se: se bebe, se comen, se toma, se fuman, se toman, se fabrica

Page 14

A Likes and dislikes: Sample answers. Felipe - Me gusta practicar el piragüismo y me encanta hacer footing, pero odio/no me gusta nada jugar al golf. Raúl - Me gusta jugar al hockey y me encanta jugar al voleibol pero odio/no me gusta nada practicar la equitación. Cisco – Me gustan las cartas y me fascina el ajedrez, pero no me atrae el deporte.

B Giving reasons: [Smiling face symbol] barato/a, divertido/a, entretenido/a, relajante, emocionante, fascinante, genial, fácil, gratis. [Unsmiling face] peligroso/a, estúpido/a, caro/a, duro/a, inútil, aburrido/a

Page 15

C The Internet: 1 She loves them **2** A laptop **3** Two of: the hard disk isn't very big, doesn't have broadband, can't download big files **4** Gets lots of junk mail **5** She goes to an Internet café **6** Reads pages from British websites, spends fifteen minutes in chat rooms with other Internet users **7** It's a Spanish social networking site **8** Have you got an account on Facebook? Would you like to invite me to be a friend?

Page 16

A Staying healthy: Joaquín B, C, F, A. Paco A, F, H, B. Alicia B, D, C

Reading for detail: a Alicia **b** Paco **c** Alicia **d** Joaquín **e** Alicia **f** Paco

Page 17

C Health issues: **C2: Verbs:** to abuse, to attack, to use, to take drugs, to inject oneself, to provoke/bring on/ induce, to relax. **Nouns:** attack, alcoholism, drug-addict, stress, smoker, withdrawal symptoms, system, substance, vein. **Adjectives:** cardiac, passive, chemical, respiratory, psychological

C3: un fumador pasivo, tabaquismo pasivo, inyectarse en una vena, provocar un ataque cardiaco o estrés psicológico, utilizar sustancias químicas, drogarse con sustancias peligrosas, atacar el sistema respiratorio

Page 18

A Special occasions: A1: 1-B, **2**-E, **3**-B, **4**-A, **5**-E, **6**-C, **7**-D, **8**-C

Page 19

B Mealtimes: A1: Dani-M, Alicia-D, Nuria-T, Paco-M, Lorenzo-D

Practice: Nombre - Ben; Comida preferida - la tortilla española; Detesta - la coliflor; Le gusta beber - zumo de fruta; Vegetariano/a - sí

Page 20

A Using technology: Ricardo - 3 Carmen - 6 Susi - 2 Alicia - 1 Gabi - 4 Pablo - 5

D Saying when and how often:

1 en verano, en otoño, en invierno **2** una vez al mes **3** tres veces a la semana **4** los lunes por la noche **5** los martes los sábados

Practice: 1 en invierno **2** en julio y agosto **3** dos veces a la semana **4** después de las clases del colegio **5** los viernes por la noche **6** los domingos

Page 21

B **New technologies – for and against:** B2: **1** La ventaja de Internet es que puedes mantenerte en contacto con amigos. **2** Lo bueno es que es posible conocer a gente de otros países y otras culturas. **3** El peligro es que hace más fácil el robo de la identidad. **4** El problema es que hace más fácil el acceso a la pornografía. **5** Me gusta Internet. Puedes mantenerte al corriente de lo que pasa. **6** Hace posible la compra para las personas confinadas en su casa. **7** Puedes ver programas de la tele cuando te convenga. **8** Lo malo es que puedes perder mucho tiempo en sitios como Twitter.

Page 22

A **Personal details:** **1**-b, **2**-c

B **Descriptions:** **1**-2, **2**-sunglasses.

C **Helping at home:** **1**-c, e. **2**-b

Page 23

D **Daily routine:** **1**-d, **2**-a, **3**-h, **4**-g, **5**-e

E **Relationships:** **1**-c, **2**-b, **3**-b, **4**-a

Page 26

B **A/De:** **1**-c, **2**-f, **3**-g, **4**-h, **5**-b, **6**-a, **7**-d, **8**-e

Page 27

E **Relative pronouns:** **a** que, **b** quién **c** lo que

Page 28

A **My home:** **1** antigua **2** pequeña **3** amueblada **4** grande **5** espacioso **6** bonita **7** verde **8** nuevo

B **Adding detail:** **1**-e, **2**-i, **3**-h, **4**-g, **5**-c, **6**-d, **7**-a, **8**-b, **9**-f

Page 29

C **My bedroom: a** - Conchi **b** - Gema **c** - Pablo **d** - Pablo **e** - Conchi **f** - Gema **g** - Gema **h** - Pablo **i** - Conchi **j** - Gema

Page 31

C **Understanding descriptions:** a, c, f, h, j

Page 32

A **In the tourist office:** **1**-i, **2**-f, **3**-j, **4**-d, **5**-g, **6**-b, **7**-a, **8**-c, **9**-h, **10**-e

Page 34

A **Talking about the weather:** En el norte está nublado y llueve. En el sur hace sol y calor. En las montañas hay tormenta y nieva. En la costa hay niebla y hace frío.

B **Forecasts:** lluvia b, f, h, l; calor e, g, j, k, m; nubes d, i; frío a, c, n

Page 35

C **The autonomous communities:** **1**-l, **2**-e, **3**-c, **4**-o, **5**-j, **6**-g, **7**-b, **8**-d, **9**-m, **10**-p, **11**-n, **12**-q, **13**-r, **14**-f, **15**-a, **16**-i, **17**-s, **18**-k, **19**-h

Practice: **1**-a, c; **2**-b, d; **3**-f; **4**-g, h

Page 37

D **Impersonal verbs:** I've got a headache. He loves football. I haven't got a fork. I need more time. I'm interested in golf. There are two biscuits left. There's bread left over.

Page 38

A **Asking where a place is: 1** Sí, hay uno en la avenida de Cádiz. **2** Sí, hay una en la avenida de Cádiz. **3** Sí, hay una en la calle Goya. **4** Sí, hay unos/servicios en la calle Sol. **5** Sí, hay uno en la plaza Mayor. **6** Sí, hay una en la plaza Mayor. **7** Sí, hay unas en la avenida de Cádiz.

A3: 1 por **2** uno **3** enfrente **4** entre **5** gracias **6** nada

Page 39

B **Directions: 1** baje la calle **2** tuerza a la izquierda **3** tome la primera a la izquierda **4** siga todo recto **5** al final de la calle **6** cruce la plaza **7** tuerza a la derecha **8** tome la segunda a la derecha **9** siga hasta el cruce **10** hasta los semáforos

B3: 1 la catedral **2** el mercado **3** la parada de autobús **4** los servicios **5** el banco

Practice: 1 Siga todo recto hasta el cruce con el paseo San Juan. Está allí, enfrente de la cafetería. **2** Siga todo recto hasta el final de la calle Goya. Tuerza a la derecha, y está allí enfrente. **3** Hay una farmacia en la calle Goya. Siga todo recto y está a la izquierda, entre El Corte Inglés y el banco. **4** Siga todo recto hasta el semáforo. Está allí, a la izquierda.

Page 40

A **In the street: 1**-f, **2**-a, **3**-h, **4**-b, **5**-i, **6**-g **7**-c, **8**-d

Page 41

B **Means of travel: 1**-f, **2**-e, **3**-c, **4**-a, **5**-g, **6**-d

C **Getting around:** Vengo en tren. Vivo bastante lejos del instituto. Es rápido y cómodo, pero caro. Tardo unos veinte minutos.

Page 42

A **Improving the environment:** **A2: a** in my opinion **b** personally **c** I think that **d** in my view/to my way of seeing **e** from my point of view

Page 43

B **Transport issues:** Leonora: circulación/tráfico, Adriano: caro Paco: aparcar

Page 44

A **My home: 1**-B, **2**-A, **3**-C

B **My town: 1**-A, C; **2**–B, C, D, F

C **Opinions:** Andrés-P, Julia-N, Karim-P+N

Page 45

D **Weather and climate: a** - on the coast; **b** - the climate, swim in the sea

D2: Winter: rain, cold, wind Summer: sunny, pleasant, not too hot

E **Transport:** 1, 3, 5

F **Environment: a** cars **b** recycle **c** simple

Page 49

E **Demonstrative adjectives and pronouns: a** este **b** esa **c** aquel **d** esta/ésta **e** esos/éstos **f** aquellas/aquéllas

Page 50

A **Invitations:** (Javi and Marifé) **1** el **2** de **3** por **4** el **5** por **6** por

Page 51

B **TV and film:** Miguel-P, Alicia-P+N, Santiago-P, Belén-P, Pablo-P+N, Teresa P+N, Eduardo-N

Page 52

A **The media and celebrities:** **1** Any three of: TV, radio, press, film **2** You are unhappy/discontented with your life **3** Entertain **4** Celebrate the talent and personality of ordinary people **5** A market **6** Any two of: wedding, children, relationships **7** To be famous **8** Any two of: sacred/holy figures, rituals, being a member of a community (which adores and venerates its stars)

Page 53

B **Fashion:** 1-b 2-c 3-c 4-c 5-b 6-b

Page 55

C **Local and out-of-town shopping:** **A** 1, 6, 7 **B** 2, 4, 5 **C** 3, 8

Page 56

A **On holiday: 1** padres **2** bonito **3** lejos **4** buena **5** mal **6** nunca **7** natación

B **Using different tenses:** **1** Paso mis vacaciones/Estoy de vacaciones en Escocia. **2** El pueblo es bonito y turístico. **3** Visito castillos, y voy de paseo/paseo por la playa y la costa. **4** Hace bastante calor, pero llueve a veces. **5** Ayer alquilé una bici. **6** El fin de semana voy a ir de excursión en barco.

Page 57

C **Restaurants:** ticks for 2, 3, 4, 6, 7

C2: De primero, quiero ensalada de tomates. Me gustaría probar la tortilla española con patatas fritas. Para mí, un helado de fresa, Quisiera agua mineral con gas.

Page 59

D **The perfect tense: 1** Has visitado **2** Has perdido **3** he probado **4** ha salido **5** ha dejado

Page 60

A **Enquiring about facilities: 1** Hotel **2** piscina **3** playa **4** habitación **5** teléfono **6** televisión **7** doce **8** ordenador

B **Handling a phone conversation: 2** Sí. ¿En qué puedo servirle? **3** Para cuándo/qué fechas, y para cuánto tiempo? **4** Muy bien. ¿Qué tipo de habitación quiere? **5** No hay problema. ¿Su nombre, por favor? **6** ¿Me lo puede deletrear?/¿Cómo se escribe, por favor? **7** Ya lo tengo, gracias. **8** Tenemos conexión Wi-Fi en el salón. **9** Tenemos también una sala de ordenadores que está abierta sin interrupción.

Page 61

C **Making a letter of complaint:** 1-F 2-D 3-C 4-B 5-G 6-A 7-H 8-I 9-J 10-E

Page 62

A **Parts of the body: 1** la cabeza **2** la nariz **3** los oídos **4** la boca **5** la muela **6** la garganta **7** los ojos **8** la espalda **9** el brazo **10** la mano **11** el dedo **12** el estómago **13** la pierna **14** el pie

Page 63

C **Lost property:** ticks for 1, 3, 4, 7

Page 64

A **Phone messages: 1**-e **2**-h **3**-f **4**-d **5**-a **6**-b **7**-g **8**-c

A3: ¿Hablo con la secretaria?, Me pone con el señor Gómez, por favor, ¡Qué pena!/fastidio/lata!, ¿Me puede llamar a las cuatro y media?, Soy Sam Thompson, de Gales, Mi número de teléfono es el 740692. El prefijo es 01745, Gracias, adiós.

Page 65

B **Mobile phones:** A-8 B-5 C-7 D-3 E-6 F-4 G-1

B3: **a**-D **b**-F **c**-D **d**-C **e**-E **f**-B

Page 66

A **Leisure:** A-3 B-2 C-1

A2: **1**-likes **2**-dislikes **3**-doesn't say **4**-likes **5**-likes

B **Illness:** Correct sentences are 2, 3, 5

Page 67

C **Eating Out:** 1-people 2-the set menu 3-(very) nice/good/tasty 4-free 5-strawberries 6-is included 7-first 8-beside/next to

D **Shopping:** Roberto-2, 4 Alicia-5

E **Accommodation: Rooms 1** not good, **2** hear TV from room next door. **Food 1** little variety, **2** mostly rice and meat

Page 70

The future and the conditional tenses: tendrá, aprenderá, habrá, será, iría, podría, querría, haría, habría

Page 71

The imperfect tense: iba, estaba, tomaba, empezábamos, tenían, gustaba, archivaba, hacía, cogía, repartía, solíamos

Page 72

A **Likes and Dislikes:** Correct sentences are 2, 3, 4, 5, 7

Page 73

B **After the exams: 1** ¡Voy a descansar un tiempo! **2** Me gustaría buscar un empleo y ganar dinero **3** Voy al volver al instituto y a seguir estudiando **4** Espero hacer Bachillerato.

Page 74

A **Part-time jobs:** 1-b, 2-f, 3-a, 4-h, 5-d, 6-e, 7-g

B **Expanding your replies:** **1** sábados **2** siete **3** nueve **4** cuatro **5** siete euros **6** interesante

Page 75

C How you spend your money:
1 Sabrina 2 Isabel 3 Isabel
4 Enrique 5 Sabrina 6 Sabrina
7 Pablo

Page 77

B Further study and training:
1-AC, 2-D, 3-BC, 4-D, 5-AD

Page 80

A Work-experience: 1-e 2-c 3-g
4-a 5-f 6-d 7-h 8-b

B Giving details: a Trabajé en una
agencia de viajes. **b** Duraron
diez días. **c** Iba en autobús y
andando. **d** ¡Tardaba casi una
hora! **e** Trabajaba de nueve a
cinco y media. **f** Sí. Había tres
descansos de veinte minutos.
g Era de una a dos. **h** Sí. En
general, era muy divertido, pero
a veces era un poco repetitivo.

Page 81

Practice: 1 En una oficina de
información y turismo. **2** Es
aburrido. **3** Preparar folletos
turísticos en el ordenador.
4 Seguir estudiando.
5 Gana bastante. **6** Un país
sudamericano/Bolivia.

Page 82

A Your CV: 1 García Morales
2 Carmen **3** 17 años
4 10.4.1984 **5** Lima, Perú
6 Peruana **7** Soltera **8** 36 741
802C **9** Calle San Agustín
18, 2ºD, 28002, Madrid
10 (91) 746 65 71 **11** Instituto
San Ignacio, Madrid (ESO,
Bachillerato) **12** Prácticas
laborales en el Hospital Juan de
Dios **13** Fotografía/ baloncesto
14 Médica

Page 83

B Job Advertisements: Begoña 3,
David 2, Juanjo 1

Page 84

A Future plans: 1 Quiero trabajar
en la enseñanza con niños
pequeños. **2** Voy a seguir
estudiando en el colegio.
3 Quisiera/Me gustaría buscar
un empleo manual. **4** Me
gustaría/Quisiera tener mi

propia empresa. **5** Quiero viajar
al extranjero. **6** Quisiera/Me
gustaría trabajar en un equipo,
en los servicios médicos.

Page 85

B Job applications: 1-e **2**-d **3**-k **4**-b
5-g **6**-c **7**-f **8**-l **9**-h

Page 86

A Concerns for the future: B-4,
C-1, D-3, E-2

A2: Ángel: preterite - pasó,
imperfect - era. Carmelina:
perfect - he resistido. Iñigo:
conditional - preferiría. Zohora:
preterite - nací.

Page 87

B Reading between the lines:
Ángel does not want to spend
ten years without any money/
income, as his father had to.
2 The village is dead. **3** He'd like
to travel a little/see the world.
4 He doesn't feel confident
enough. **5** It makes her cry.
6 Carmelina feels unsure/
uncertain (of her ability to resist
the pressure from her friends).

Page 88

A School: Size - Juan, Type -
Rosario, Number of pupils -
Rosario, Ages of pupils - Rosario,
Buildings - Juan

B Uniform: A - trousers **B** - grey
C - shirt **D** - lilac/purple

B2: A - boring **B** - comfortable

C Facilities: German - second left,
English - first right, Art - end of
corridor

Page 89

D Subjects: A - likes **B** - likes
C - doesn't like **D** - doesn't like

D2: A – Teacher is very amusing/
funny. **B** – Gets bad marks

E Jobs: Father - used to work in a
shop, now works in a factory.
Mother - works as an air hostess/
in the airport, would not like to
work in an office.

F Work and Future Plans: 1 - Is he
(still) working in the restaurant?
2 - Learning languages. **3** - No

longer working in a shop/no
longer a shop assistant. **4** - Be an
air hostess, travel a lot. **5** - He
used to look after children.
6 - He gets on well with people.
7 Wants to be a PE/sports
teacher, he needs more
experience.

Exam questions and model answers

Page 91

Question 1: 1 usual holiday **2**
means of travel **3** weather
4 opinion **5** future plans

Extra Practice: 1 friends **2** a
week

Question 2: 1-I **2** -F **3**-L **4**-G
5-E **6**-B

Question 3: 1 past **2** past
3 present **4** future **5** present

Page 95

Question 1: 1 1d, 2a, 3e, 4c

Question 2 1-P+N, 2-N, 3-P+N.

Question 3 1E, 2F, 3A, 4B, 5C

Page 96

1Q *four (típico, cómodo, tranquilo,
maravillosas), plus two past
participles of verbs used as
adjectives:* situado and cubierta.
*Adjectives usually come after the
noun. They can be joined with
y/e (and).*

Your turn! Visité un pueblo
antiguo e interesante, enclavado
al pie de la montaña bonita y
verde con vistas estupendas
hacia la sierra cubierta de nubes
blancas.

Page 97

2Q Personalmente, me parece, por
un lado, por otra. Your turn!
A mi modo de ver el iPod me
parece divertido. Por una parte,
es muy entretenido pero por otra
es un artículo de lujo.

3Q primero (first), luego (then,
después de (after –ing), más
tarde (later), finalmente
~(finally). Your turn! En primer
lugar, llegamos al estadio a
tiempo. Pero luego, después de

pasar 3 horas en una cola, nos dijeron que hubo un problema con las entradas. Dos horas más tarde, entramos en el estadio por fin.

Complete the Grammar 98–105

A/some: un hermano, una hermana, unos hombres, unas mujeres

The: el tío, la tía, los chicos, las chicas

Plural nouns: 30 libros, 15 mesas. 4 tablones, 3 ordenadores, 8 luces, 2 estantes, 5 pósters

Adjectives: italiana, catalana, escocesa, española, marrón, rosa/rosas

Gustar: Me gusta el dibujo. No me gusta la historia. Me gustan las matemáticas. No me gustan los deberes.

Comparatives: más que, menos que, tan … como. Tanto ruido, tanta polución, tantos coches, tantas chicas.

Indirect object pronouns:
I like - me gusta(n), you like - te gusta(n), he/she/you likes - le gusta(n), we like - nos gusta(n), you like - os gusta(n), they/you like - les gusta(n)

Present tense: (tú) hablas, (él, ella, usted) habla, (ellos, ellas, usted) hablan, (yo) como, (nosotros/as) comemos, (yo) vivo, (tú) vives, (vosotros/as) vivís

Irregular present tense: dar - doy, conocer - conozco, hacer - hago, poner - pongo, saber - sé, salir - salgo, traer - traigo, ver - veo

Ir: vas, vamos, van

Tener: tengo, tiene, tenéis

Estar: estoy, estás, estamos, están

Ser: eres, es, sois, son

Use **estar** to indicate position, and temporary moods. Use **ser** for describing people, places, things.

The immediate future: Use the verb **ir** followed by a, and the **infinitive** of another verb.

A/De

a When followed by **el** it becomes **al**.

b When followed by **el** it becomes **del**.

Reflexive verbs: (yo) me, (tú) te, (él, ella, usted) se, (ellos, ellas, ustedes) se

Question words: ¿dónde?, ¿cuánto?, ¿cómo?, ¿qué?, ¿cuándo?, ¿quién(es)?, ¿por qué?

Positive commands: (tú) come, escribe; (usted) hable, coma; escriba; (tú) tuerce, sigue; (usted) cruce, coja, siga

The perfect tense: dejado, comido, salido, he escrito, he hecho, he puesto, he roto, he visto

The regular preterite tense: yo hablé, tú hablaste, él, ella, usted habló, ellos, ellas, ustedes hablaron; tú comiste, nosotros comimos, vosotros comisteis; yo viví, él, ella, usted vivió, ellos, ellas, ustedes vivieron

Irregular preterite verbs: ser/ir - fuiste, fuimos, fueron; **dar** - di, dio, disteis

The 'pretérito grave' stems: yo -estuve, hic-, pud-, pus-, quis-, tuv-, vin-; tú -iste, nosotros -imos, ellos, ellas, ustedes -ieron

Stem/radical changing verbs: o changes to ue, yo puedo, I am able to; u changes to ue, tú juegas, you play; e changes to ie, él prefiere, he prefers; e changes to i, ellas piden, they ask for.

Direct object pronouns: singulars - te, lo, la; **plurals** - nos, los, las

Direct object pronouns usually come **before** the verb.

They can be added on to the **end** of an infinitive.

Demonstrative adjectives: (this, fs) esta, (that, ms) ese, (that there, fs) aquella, (these, mpl) estos, (those, fpl) esas, (those there, mpl) aquellos

Demonstrative pronouns (this/that one, these/those ones) are the same as the adjectives above, but have an **accent** on the first 'e'.

Verbs of obligation: (have to, must) tener que, (ought to, should) deber, (one has to) hay que

Se … : se + third person of the verb …; se come, se bebe, se escribe

The regular imperfect tense: (tú) hablabas, (nosotros) hablábamos, (ellos, ellas, ustedes) hablaban; (yo) bebía, (él, ella, usted) bebía, (vosotros) bebíais, (tú) vivías, (nosotros) vivíamos, (ellos, ellas, ustedes) vivían

Irregular imperfect tense verbs

Ir: ibas, iba, ibais, iban **Ser:** era, era, éramos, eran **Ver:** veías, veía, veíamos, veían

The gerund and continuous tenses:
-ar verbs: -ando   (andando)
-er verbs: -iendo   (comiendo)
-ir verbs: -iendo   (escribiendo)

Present continuous: use the present tense of the verb **estar** + gerund

Imperfect continuous: use the **imperfect** tense of the verb estar + gerund

Which tense?: (present), Vivo; present, Soy; imperfect, iba; perfect, he perdido; preterite, dejé; immediate future, voy a llamar

The future and conditional tenses: The future tense indicates what **will** happen.

The conditional indicates what **would** happen. The endings are the same for **-ar**, **-er**, **-ir** verbs.

Future: (tú) hablarás, (nosotros) hablaremos, (ellos, ellas, ustedes) hablarán

Conditional: (yo) hablaría, (él, ella, usted) hablaría, (vosotros) hablaríais

Irregular future/conditional stems: har-, podr-, pondr-, querr-, tendr-, vendr-

Ser/estar: ser - 2 jobs/professions; **estar** - 1 temporary states; 3 position/place

Negative commands: (tú) no comas, no escribas, (usted) no hable, no coma, no escriba, (vosotros/as) no comáis, no escribáis, (ustedes) no hablen, no coman, no escriban

Impersonal verbs: to hurt - doler; to delight - encantar; to be lacking - faltar; to be necessary - hacer falta; to interest - interesar; to remain; be left over - quedar; to be an excess of - sobrar

Me duele la espalda; Te encanta el deporte, ¿no?; Le falta un cuchillo; Nos hace falta más dinero; Os interesa mucho el tenis, creo; Quedan tres manzanas. Sobra vino.

Adverbs: To form adverbs, take the masculine form of the **adjective**. Now make it **feminine** and add -mente: rápido, rápida, rápidamente; lento, lenta, lentamente; fácil, fácil, fácilmente

Well - bien; badly - mal; slowly - despacio

There are two words for quickly: rápido, rápidamente

Check your grammar in the exam

Gender of nouns: do I need **el**, **la**, **los** or **las**? Should it be **un**, **una**, **unos**, **unas**?

The word for 'to/at' is **a**; followed by **el**, it becomes **al**

The word for 'of/from' is **de**: followed by **el**, it becomes **del**.

Endings on adjectives: masculine, feminine, singular, plural

Endings on verbs: is this the correct tense?

Impersonal verbs like **gustar** need an indirect object pronoun: should it be **me**, **te**, **le**, **nos**, **os**, **les**?

Direct object pronouns: use **lo, le, la, los, las** for people, and **lo, la, los, las** for things.

Vocabulary extra

Connectives: moreover, apart from, given that, that is, on the one hand, on the other hand, without a doubt/doubtless.

Negatives: nunca/jamás, ni … ni, nada, ningún/a, nadie, no … sino, tampoco.

Greetings and exclamations: (First column) ¡Bienvenido!, ¡Buena suerte!, ¡Cuidado!, ¡Felices Pascuas/Semana Santa!, ¡Felicidades!, ¡Feliz Año Nuevo!, ¡Feliz Navidad!, ¡Ojo! ¡Que aproveche!, ¡Qué asco!, ¡Qué (+ adjective/noun)! ¡Qué desastre!, ¡Qué pena!

(Second column) Enough! Have a good journey! Of course! Congratuations! Have a good holiday!, Congratulations, Happy Birthday!, Happy Saint's Day! ,Bravo! ,Have a good time! ,How nice/great!, How awful! What a shame!

Common Verbs: dar, deber, estar, ser, hacer, hay, hay que, ir, poder, querer, tener, tener que, pasar, oír, poner, tener lugar, venir, volver, volverse/hacerse, irse, subir, bajar, encender, apagar, pensar, preferir.

Expressions with tener (to have …): (First column) tener … años, tener calor, tener cuidado, tener éxito, tener frío, tener ganas (de).

(Second column) to be hungry, to be afraid, to be right, to be thirsty, to be sleepy, to be lucky

Adverbs: (First column) for a long time, often, sometimes, many times, up/down, over there, here, although, rather/quite, almost, too (much), quickly/hurriedly

(Second column) desgraciadamente, inmediatamente, sobre todo, más, muy, tal vez/quizá(s), realmente, recientemente, siempre, todavía, ya, enseguida.

Quantities: una botella de, una caja de, una docena de, un kilo de, medio kilo/litro, una lata de, un litro de, un paquete de, un pedazo/trozo de, una rebanada de, un tarro de, un envase/una tarrina de, la mitad

de, un quarto de, un tercio de, doble, un poco de, suficiente, solamente/sólo, varios/as

Expressions of time and connecting words: a partir de, ahora mismo, al día siguiente, de vez en cuando, ayer, desde, más tarde, después, anteayer, pasado mañana, el fin de semana, o, pero, pues

Tapescript

LISTENING SECTION A
(pp. 22–23)

A Personal Details

1 La estación está en la calle Cuenca. Cuenca se escribe C-U-E-N-C-A. La calle Cuenca, C-U-E-N-C-A.

2 Su cumpleaños es el dieciséis de enero.

B Descriptions

1 Era bastante alto, rubio y llevaba gafas. Era muy simpático.

2 Siempre lleva gafas de sol.

C Helping at Home

1 Para ayudar a mis padres, paso la aspiradora, y saco la basura.

2 Me gusta más preparar la comida porque es más divertido.

D Daily Routine

Me llamo Susana y estoy en el cuarto de la ESO. Cada día me levanto a las siete y voy al colegio. Llego al colegio a las ocho y las clases empiezan a las ocho y media. A la una, almuerzo en casa de un amigo y vuelvo a clase a las dos y media. Las clases terminan a las cuatro, pero normalmente hago mis deberes en la biblioteca con mis amigos hasta las cinco.

E Relationships

[Hombre] Ahora hablamos con Lucía. Tú tienes un problema con tus padres, Lucía, ¿verdad?

[Lucía] Sí. No me llevo muy bien con mis padres de momento porque no me dejan salir con mis amigos. No es justo porque yo soy la única de mi grupo de amigos que no puede salir.

[Hombre] ¿Lucía, adónde van tus amigos cuando salen?

[Lucía] Van a la discoteca, a cafeterías y a bares. Lo normal.

[Hombre] ¿Y cuántos años tienes, Lucía?

[Lucía] Tengo quince años, pero mis amigos tienen diecisiete o dieciocho años.

[Hombre] Y los amigos de tu clase del instituto, ¿no sales con ellos?

[Lucía] Es que ellos no salen. Son muy aburridos.

LISTENING SECTION B
(pp. 44–45)

A My home

1 Vivo en una casa adosada. Mi casa está cerca del instituto, al lado del supermercado.

2 Pienso que mi casa es bastante antigua pero cómoda. - No es fea pero no es muy bonita tampoco.

3 Lo mejor de mi casa es que está cerca del instituto, así que no tengo que levantarme pronto.

B My town

1 Hay discotecas, bares y se puede ir a la playa.

2 Para visitar hay el castillo y la catedral o también se puede ir a la piscina, y por la noche se puede salir con amigos. Para divertirse hay una gama enorme de restaurantes, bares y discotecas. Hay mucho que hacer.

C Opinions

[Andrés] Hay muchas cosas de interés en la zona donde yo vivo. Hay un cine, restaurantes y también hay parques muy bonitos, polideportivos fantásticos y tiendas muy buenas.

[Julia] No hay muchas distracciones para los jóvenes en mi pueblo. Hay polideportivos, tiendas y piscinas, pero hay que tener dinero. Los jóvenes sólo pueden ir al parque gratis o reunirse en las calles, y esto no está bien.

[Andrés] A mi amigo Karim, le gusta su pueblo porque todos sus amigos viven cerca y es muy bonito. Lo malo es que no hay mucho para los jóvenes – sólo un campo de fútbol y a él no le interesa nada el deporte.

D Weather and Climate

1 En el futuro me gustaría vivir en la costa, en España porque prefiero el clima y me gusta nadar en el mar.

2 En invierno hace mal tiempo- es decir, llueve, hace frío y hace mucho viento. Pero en verano hace sol y para mí es agradable porque no hace demasiado calor.

E Transport

Quiero un billete de ida y vuelta a Madrid.

Muy bien.

Primera clase, por favor.

Aquí tiene.

¿De qué andén sale?

Andén numero siete.

¿Cuánto cuesta?

Cinco euros con cuarenta y seis.

¿A qué hora sale el tren?

Sale a las diez, pero va con quince minutos de retraso

F Environment

Hay demasiados coches. Y todavía hay mucha gente que no recicla y eso es una cosa sencilla que todos podemos hacer.

LISTENING SECTION C
(pp. 66–67)

A Leisure

1 El fin de semana pasado fui al cine con mi hermano menor el sábado por la tarde. Vi la nueva película de Harry Potter - era divertida. El domingo tuve que estudiar mucho porque los exámenes son muy importantes. ¡Qué aburrido!

2 Prefiero las películas de acción porque son emocionantes. No me gustan nada las películas románticas porque son aburridas y falsas. Mi película favorita se llama Bourne Identity.

Aparte de los libros del colegio, no leo mucho porque en mi tiempo libre prefiero escuchar música.

Me gusta la música pop porque me encanta bailar, me encanta escuchar la radio y hay unos cantantes muy buenos. Mi grupo favorito es The Beatles porque es un grupo muy inteligente y su música es muy popular.

B Illness

No me siento bien.

¿Te duele la cabeza?

Sí, me duele mucho.

¿Quieres tomar unas pastillas?

Sí por favor.

Debes ir a la cama para descansar.

Estoy de acuerdo, pero ¿qué vamos a hacer esta tarde?

No tengo planes especiales para esta tarde.

Pues, voy a dormir un rato.

C Eating Out

¿Para cuántas personas?

Pause

¿Quieren el menú del día?

Pause

Las gambas al ajillo están muy ricas.

Pause

El pan es gratis.

Pause

Lo siento no quedan más fresas.

Pause

El servicio está incluído.

Pause

Están en la primera planta al lado de los teléfonos.

D Shopping

[Alicia] ¿Adónde vas, Roberto?

[Roberto] Voy a la tienda de discos porque quiero comprarme el nuevo disco compacto de mi grupo favorito. ¿Y tú Alicia?

[Alicia] Voy al centro comercial. Necesito un vestido.

[Roberto] Después, voy a la pastelería. Necesito comprar un pastel porque hoy es el cumpleaños de mi madre."

E Accommodation

¿Les ha gustado su estancia en el hotel?

Pues, las habitaciones no son buenas, se puede oír la televisión de la habitación de al lado. En cuanto a la comida, hay muy poca variedad de platos. Generalmente no hay más que arroz con carne."

LISTENING SECTION D (pp.88–89)

A School

[Juan] Es un instituto grande.

[Roasario] Es un instituto mixto. También es un instituto de idiomas y de la comunidad.

[Rosario] Hay más o menos mil estudiantes de entre trece y dieciocho años.

[Juan] Los edificios son grandes y sucios.

B Uniform

1   Tengo que llevar un pantalón negro, un jersey gris, una camisa blanca y una corbata negra, lila y gris. Pienso que el uniforme es aburrido pero cómodo.

C Facilities

El aula de alemán es la segunda a la izquierda, el aula de inglés es la primera a la derecha y el aula de dibujo está al final del pasillo.

D Subjects

1   Personalmente prefiero las humanidades. Por ejemplo, me encanta la historia porque es interesante. Me gusta también la geografía porque el profe es muy divertido. Odio las matemáticas porque saco malas notas. Tampoco me gusta mucho el dibujo porque es muy aburrido.

E Jobs

Antes mi padre trabajaba en una tienda en el centro de la ciudad, pero ahora mi padre trabaja en una fábrica cerca del hospital. Mi madre no trabaja en la ciudad. Es azafata, y tiene que ir al aeropuerto para coger el avión. Le gusta mucho su trabajo porque le encanta viajar al extranjero, pero no le gustaría nada trabajar en una oficina.

F Work and Future Plans

[Cristina] ¿Trabajas todavía en el restaurante Paco?

[Paco] No, tengo un nuevo empleo. De momento trabajo en la recepción de un gran hotel en la playa. Soy recepcionista. Voy a empezar a estudiar idiomas porque en el futuro me gustaría trabajar en el extranjero ¿Y tú Cristina? ¿Sigues trabajando en la tienda del centro principal?

[Cristina] No, ya no soy dependienta. Ahora estudio en la universidad – estoy estudiando idiomas porque me gustaría ser azafata. Me gustaría viajar mucho en el futuro. ¿Qué hace tu hermano Ignacio?

[Paco] Como sabes antes cuidaba niños. Le gustaba mucho, porque se relaciona bien con los jóvenes. De momento está trabajando en el polideportivo porque quiere ser profesor de deporte y necesita más experiencia.

EXAM LISTENING
(pp. 90–91)

1 Tasks with Grids

[1] Prefiero ver las películas en la tele.

[2] Me gusta jugar todos los deportes pero mi favorito es el fútbol porque soy muy bueno. Juego en un equipo todos los sábados.

[3] Sí me gusta el cine pero es bastante caro. Normalmente voy al cine una vez al mes.

[4] El sábado por la mañana fui de compras con mi mamá y compré un vestido nuevo.

[5] No está mal la informática. Me gusta navegar por internet, y escribir a mis amigos por e-mail [correo-electrónico], pero odio jugar con el ordenador, es muy aburrido.

2 Choosing the correct words

Tengo un trabajo a tiempo parcial. Soy camarera y trabajo en un café cerca de mi casa. Trabajo los sábados de diez a cuatro. Traigo bebidas y comidas para los clientes. El trabajo es duro y me duelen los pies al final del día pero la gente es muy amable.

Question 1

[1] Normalmente voy a Escocia.

[2] Fuimos en avión.

[3] Hizo sol y mucho calor.

[4] No me gustaron mucho porque era aburrido.

[5] Después de los exámenes voy a irme de vacaciones con mis amigos. Vamos a ir una semana a Benidorm.

Question 2

Las reglas en mi escuela son muy estrictas. Yo creo que las reglas son necesarias pero algunas son estupidas, por ejemplo no está permitido mascar chicle dentro de la clase. Yo estudio en una escuela pública y tengo que llevar uniforme. Los uniformes son un poco aburridos."

Question 3

Hace siete años vivía en las afueras de la cuidad. A mí no me gustaba porque estaba demasiado contaminada. Me gustaba más cuando vivíamos en un pueblo tranquilo. Mis abuelos viven en el campo y me encanta pasar tiempo allí. Ahora vivimos en la costa y es mucho mejor pero me encantaría vivir en las montañas.

Last-minute learner

- **The next four pages give you the key vocabulary across the whole subject in the smallest possible space.**
- **You can use these pages as a final check.**
- **You can also use them as you revise as a way to check your learning.**
- **You can cut them out for quick and easy reference.**

Numbers

1	uno	11	once	21	veintiuno	31	treinta y uno	101	ciento uno
2	dos	12	doce	22	veintidós	32	treinta y dos	200	doscientos
3	tres	13	trece	23	veintitrés	40	cuarenta	300	trescientos
4	cuatro	14	catorce	24	veinticuatro	50	cincuenta	400	cuatrocientos
5	cinco	15	quince	25	veinticinco	60	sesenta	500	quinientos
6	seis	16	dieciséis	26	veintiséis	70	setenta	600	seiscientos
7	siete	17	diecisiete	27	veintisiete	80	ochenta	700	setecientos
8	ocho	18	dieciocho	28	veintiocho	90	noventa	800	ochocientos
9	nueve	19	diecinueve	29	veintinueve	100	cien	900	novecientos
10	diez	20	veinte	30	treinta			1000	mil

Days of the week

lunes	*Monday*
martes	*Tuesday*
miércoles	*Wednesday*
jueves	*Thursday*
viernes	*Friday*
sábado	*Saturday*
domingo	*Sunday*
el fin de semana	*weekend*

Months of the year

enero	*January*	julio	*July*
febrero	*February*	agosto	*August*
marzo	*March*	septiembre	*September*
abril	*April*	octubre	*October*
mayo	*May*	noviembre	*November*
junio	*June*	diciembre	*December*

Me and my family (pp. 2–3, 6)

- Me presento. Me llamo (John Brown). Mi nombre/apellido se escribe (J-O-H-N). Tengo (quince) años. Mi cumpleaños es el (quince) de (mayo). De nacionalidad, soy (escocés). Soy (alto), y (delgado). Tengo los ojos (azules) y el pelo (corto, marrón y liso). Tengo pecas. Llevo (gafas, lentes de contacto/lentillas).
- ¿Cúantas personas hay en tu familia? En mi familia, somos (seis) personas. Mis padres están (divorciados) y vivo con mi (madre), mi (padrastro), mis dos hermanos que se llaman (David) y (Chris) y mi hermana, que se llama (Alison).
- ¡Hola! ¿Qué tal? Fenomenal, estupendo, regular/voy tirando, no muy bien, fatal. Te/le presento a mi (madre, mejor amigo). Encantado/a de conocerte/le. ¡Pasa/pase! ¡Bienvenido/a!). Muchas gracias por su hospitalidad.

Interests and hobbies (pp. 12, 14–15)

- ¿Qué deportes practicas? En mi tiempo libre, juego (al fútbol) y (al baloncesto). ¿Qué te gusta hacer (en invierno/verano?) En verano, practico (el atletismo) y (el piragüismo). En (invierno), me gusta (hacer judo), y (escuchar música).
- ¿Qué te gusta hacer en tu tiempo libre? Me encanta (navegar por Internet) porque es (interesante) pero no me gusta mucho (ver la tele) — es (aburrido). ¿Tocas algún instrumento? No toco ningún instrumento, pero me gustaría aprender a tocar (la batería). Toco (la guitarra) un poco. ¿Te gustaría (jugar, salir) con nosotros? Sí, con mucho gusto.

Home (pp. 24, 28–29)

- ¿Dónde vives? Vivo en (Sherington), (una ciudad) en el (noroeste) de (Inglaterra). Mi (casa) está (en una urbanización) en las afueras. Vivo en (una casa adosada) de (dos) plantas. Abajo hay (la cocina, el salón, el comedor, y el lavadero), y arriba hay (el cuarto de baño y tres dormitorios). Delante hay (un jardín pequeño y un garaje), y detrás está (el patio) y (un jardín más grande).

My bedroom (pp. 24, 29)

- ¿Tienes tu propio dormitorio? Sí, tengo mi propio dormitorio. No, tengo que compartir con (mi hermana). Mi dormitorio es (bastante pequeño), y (pintado/empapelado) en (azul y verde). Hay una ventana que da (al jardín). Detrás de la puerta está (la cama), y (una mesilla de noche) con (una lámpara). Debajo de la ventana, hay (un escritorio) donde (hago mis deberes). Hay también un guardarropa y un tocador para mis cosas, y un estante para mis libros y CDs.

Daily routine (pp. 8–9, 19)

- ¿A qué hora te levantas? Me levanto (a las siete) (entresemana, el fin de semana). ¿Qué llevas para ir al instituto? Llevo (un uniforme: un pantalón gris ...) ¿Cómo vas al instituto? Voy (en autobús), mi (padre) me lleva en coche. ¿A qué hora sales de casa? Salgo (a las ocho). ¿Cuánto tiempo tardas en llegar? Tardo (veinte) minutos.
- ¿A qué hora empiezan las clases? Empiezan (a las nueve). ¿Cuántas clases hay por día? Hay (seis). ¿Cuánto tiempo dura cada clase? Las clases duran (una hora). ¿Cuándo hay recreos? Hay recreos (a las once) y (a la una). ¿A qué hora terminan las clases? Terminan (a las cuatro). ¿Dónde comes al mediodía? Como (en la cantina). Vuelvo a casa para comer.
- ¿Cuándo vuelves a casa por la tarde? Vuelvo a (las cuatro y media).
- ¿Cuántas horas de deberes haces? Hago (tres) horas de deberes. ¿Qué te gusta hacer por la tarde? Me gusta (ver la tele.) ¿A qué hora te acuestas? Me acuesto a (las once).
- ¿Qué diferencias hay en tu rutina de lunes a viernes y el fin de semana? El (sábado) (me levanto tarde), y por la noche (salgo con mis amigos). Vamos a la (bolera, pista de hielo).

Meals and mealtimes (pp. 18–19)

- ¿A qué hora (desayunas, comes, cenas)? (Desayuno, como, ceno) a (las ocho). ¿Dónde sueles cenar? Suelo (cenar, comer) en (el comedor, la cocina, delante de la tele). ¿Qué tipo de comida te gusta? Me gusta (la carne) y me encantan (las pastas). Soy vegetariano/a. Soy alérgico/a a (la leche). (Odio, detesto, no aguanto) (las verduras).

School subjects, buildings, next year (pp. 68–69, 76–77)

- En total, estudio (ocho) asignaturas: (cinco) obligatorios y (tres) optativos. Estudio (la lengua y literatura ...). Me gusta mucho (el dibujo) porque es (fácil), (la profesora) es (divertida) y (saco buenas notas). Odio (la física) porque soy muy flojo/a en esta asignatura.
- Mi instituto es (bastante grande) y (moderno). Tiene muchas aulas, laboratorios, (dos) cocinas, (tres) sala(s) de ordenadores, una biblioteca, un patio, un gimnasio y un campo de deporte. Después de los exámenes, voy a (seguir mis estudios) aquí y (hacer los A levels). En verano, quiero (descansar un rato). Me gustaría (ganar dinero) y (pasarlo bien).

Asking the way (pp. 36, 38–39)

- ¿Hay (un bar/una farmacia) por aquí? Sí, hay (uno/una) en (la Plaza Mayor).
- ¿Por dónde se va al (castillo)? Tome/coja (la primera) a la (izquierda), tuerza (a la derecha), cruce (el puente), siga todo recto hasta (los semáforos, el final de la calle) y está allí, (enfrente de la comisaría).

Travel and transport (pp. 25, 40–41, 43)

- Quisiera/quiero comprar un billete (sencillo, de ida y vuelta) para (Burgos), de (segunda) clase, y (no fumador). ¿Cuánto cuesta (un bonobús?). ¿A qué hora llega (el tren de Marbella)? ¿A qué hora sale (el autocar para Madrid)? ¿De qué andén sale? ¿Hay que cambiar/hacer transbordo? ¿Cuánto tiempo tarda en llegar? ¿Hay que pagar un suplemento? ¿Dónde puedo (dejar la maleta, comprar una revista)? (La consigna, el quiosco) está (allí).

Weather (pp. 25, 34–35)

- ¿Qué tiempo hace? Hace buen/mal tiempo. ¿Qué dice el pronóstico? Hace/hará (frío, calor, mucho sol, viento).
  Hay/habrá (lluvia, neblina, niebla, granizo, tormenta). Llueve, nieva. El cielo está (despejado, nublado).

Home town. Tourism (pp. 25, 30–31)

- Mi (barrio) es (antiguo) pero (ruidoso). Para divertirse hay (el cine). Para comprar (hay el centro comercial). La gente es (simpática) pero/y (no) hay mucho para (los jóvenes). De día, se puede (acampar, visitar ..., explorar ...). De noche, se puede (ir a la discoteca). Mi ciudad ideal tendría (más lugares verdes, buenas instalaciones, más distracciones). Lo bueno es que (es bonito). Lo malo es que (no hay nada para los jóvenes). El problema es que hay mucho/a (desempleo, basura, ruido).

Holidays (p. 56)

- Fui a (España) en (avión) con (mi familia). Pasé/
pasamos (quince días) en (un hotel) cerca de (la
playa). (El hotel) era (cómodo) y la comida era
(buena).
- De día, fui (a la playa) donde tomé el sol y nadé
(en el mar). Un día, hice/hicimos una excursión (en
autocar) a (la sierra). Me gustó mucho (el ambiente)
y (el tiempo): lo pasé bomba/me divertí mucho. Algo
que no me gustó fue (la basura en las calles).

Accommodation (pp. 58, 60–61)

- ¿Dónde está la Oficina de Turismo? ¿Tiene (un
folleto sobre la ciudad, una lista de hoteles, un
horario de autobuses)? ¿A qué hora se abre/cierra (el
museo?). Estoy/estamos aquí de vacaciones. ¿Qué
hay que ver en (la ciudad/región)?
- ¿Tiene habitaciones libres? Quisiera reservar (una
habitación individual) para esta noche/(dos noches)
desde el (cinco) de (julio) hasta el (siete). ¿El
desayuno/el almuerzo está incluido? ¿A qué hora se
sirve (la cena)? Quisiera una habitación con (balcón,
vista del mar). ¿Hay sitio para (una tienda familiar)?
¿Dónde se puede (aparcar, dejar la basura, cocinar)?
Firme la ficha por favor.

Restaurants (pp. 47, 57)

- ¿Me/Nos trae el menú/la carta/la lista de vinos, por
favor? ¿Qué quiere tomar (de primero, de segundo,
de postre, para beber)? Quisiera, para mi, para mi
(amigo/a) ... ¿Qué hay para vegetarianos? ¿Qué es ...
exactamente?
¿Contiene ...? El (plato)/la (cuchara) está sucio/a.
Falta un (tenedor)/una (taza).
- ¿Me/nos trae más agua/pan por favor? ¿El servicio
está incluido? ¿Se puede pagar con tarjeta de
crédito?

Feeling ill (p. 62)

- No me siento/encuentro bien. ¿Qué te/le pasa?
Tengo (un catarro, tos, naúseas, fiebre). Me duele
el (brazo)/la garganta. Me duelen los (pies)/las
(muelas). ¿Desde hace cuánto tiempo no te sientes/
se siente bien? Desde ayer, desde hace (dos) días.
Tome (este járabe, esta medicina, estas pastillas,
estos antibióticos), ponga (esta crema, estas tiritas).
Hay que tomar (dos) cucharaditas (tres) veces al día.
¿Puede venir a verme mañana?

Lost property (p. 63)

- He perdido/Acabo de perder mi (bolsa, máquina
fotográfica, mochila). Me han robado (el monedero).
¿Dónde lo/la perdió? Creo que lo/la perdí (en
el cine). ¿Cómo lo/la perdió? Estaba (viendo la
película, mirando la tele, hablando con mis amigos).
Mi (bolsa) estaba en (el suelo, mi silla, a mi lado).
No sé cómo/qué ocurrió exactamente.
- ¿Cómo era? Era (azul), de (cuero) y bastante
(pequeño). ¿Qué contenía? Contenía (mis llaves,
mi pasaporte, mi monedero, mi billete de avión).
¿Puede usted volver mañana? Lo siento, voy a volver
a (Gran Bretaña).

Household chores (p. 9)

- ¿Tienes que ayudar en casa? ¿Qué tienes que hacer?
Tengo que (hacer mi cama) (todos los días, el fin
de semana). ¿Qué tiene que hacer tu (hermano)?
— Tiene que (lavar/fregar los platos). ¿Hay algún
quehacer que no te guste?
- Odio/detesto (poner la mesa) porque es (aburrido,
pesado).

Healthy living (pp. 12, 16–17)

- ¿Qué haces/que hay que hacer para (estar sano/a, en
forma) ¿Qué vas a hacer tú? Hago/voy a hacer (más)
ejercicio, como/voy a seguir un régimen sano). Hay
que (beber menos alcohol). Se debe (dormir siete
horas al día). Hace falta (respetar el cuerpo). Sería
mejor/es importante no (fumar, emborracharse). Es
(peligroso/dañino) (tomar drogas). Es (bueno) para
la salud (evitar demasiado estrés, tomar comida
nutritiva).

Going out, TV and films (pp. 47, 50–51)

- ¿Qué ponen el la tele/el cine? Ponen (una película
de ciencia-ficción).
- ¿Qué tipo de programa te gusta más? Me gustan
(los dibujos animados). No me gustan mucho
(los documentales). ¿Ves mucho la tele? Veo (dos)
horas al día, más/menos el fin de semana. Soy muy
aficionado/a a las telenovelas.
- ¿Cuánto cuestan las entradas? ¿A qué hora empieza/
termina (la sesión)? ¿Te gustaría ir (al cine)? Sí,
buena idea. No puedo. Tengo que (hacer los
deberes, cuidar a mi hermano/a). No me interesa
mucho. No tengo (ganas, tiempo, dinero). ¿A qué
hora nos vemos? ¿Si nos vemos a (las ocho)?

Contacting others (pp. 58, 64–65)

- ¡Diga! ¡Dígame! ¡Oiga! ¿Está (Raúl)? ¿Me pone con
(Ana)? ¿De parte de quién? De parte (del Señor
Alonso). Está comunicando. No contesta. ¿Cuál es el
número/prefijo? ¿Qué número hay que marcar? Es el
(92. 22. 51. 67).
- ¿Puedo dejar un recado?

Shopping (pp. 46, 54–55)

- ¿Dónde puedo comprar (un cinturón)? Busco (una
camiseta) ¿Tiene (gafas de sol)? ¿Se venden (cajas de
turrón)? ¿Hay pan (fresco)? Lo siento, no queda(n).
Quisiera (cien gramos) de (queso), (una lata) de
(tomates). ¿Me pone/da (un kilo de manzanas) por
favor?
- ¿Qué tamaño? Grande, pequeño, mediano. ¿Qué
talla usa? La (40). ¿Qué número calza? El (38). No
me queda(n) bien, no me va(n) bien. Es demasiado
(estrecho/a, ancho/a, largo/a, corto/a). No me gusta
el color.
- Me lo/la/los/las llevo.
- ¿Es todo? Sí, es todo. ¿Algo más? No, nada más,
gracias. ¿Tiene cambio? No, lo siento, no tengo
cambio. Sólo tengo un billete de (50) euros. ¿Se
puede pagar con (un cheque, con tarjeta de crédito,
en metálico/efectivo).

Part–time jobs (pp. 69, 74–75)

- ¿Tienes algún empleo? ¿Cuándo trabajas? Trabajo todos los días, el fin de semana desde (las ocho) hasta (la una). ¿Cuántas horas trabajas? Trabajo (seis horas) al día. ¿Cuándo empiezas/terminas? Empiezo/termino a (la una)
- ¿Cuánto ganas? Gano (tres libras esterlinas) por hora/al día. ¿Qué opinas del trabajo? Es (interesante) pero (mal pagado).

Work experience (pp. 78, 80–81)

- ¿Dónde hiciste tu experiencia laboral? La hice/trabajé en (una oficina).
- ¿Cuánto tiempo duró? Duró (diez) días.
- ¿Cómo ibas a tu lugar de trabajo? Iba (andando).
- ¿Cuánto tiempo tardabas en llegar? Tardaba unos (20) minutos.
- ¿Cómo era el horario? Empezaba/ terminaba a las (nueve).
- ¿Qué teniás que hacer? Tenía que (archivar, coger el teléfono).
- ¿Te gustó? Lo bueno era que (la gente era simpática), lo malo era que (el trabajo era repetitivo). Me divertí/me aburrí mucho.

Character and relationships (pp. 3, 10–11)

- De carácter, ¿cómo eres? Soy (amable) y (un poco perezoso). ¿Cómo es tu (padre/madre)? Mi (padre/madre) es (simpático/a). ¿Cuáles son las características de (un/a buen/a amigo/a)? Él/ella debe ser (honrado/a).
- ¿Qué tal las relaciones en tu famila? Son buenas/malas.
  ¿Te llevas bien con (tu hermano)? (No) me llevo bien con (mi hermana) porque (me irrita, me fastidia, me hace subir por las paredes). Me enfado con él, ella, mi (hermana).
- Su (comportamiento, conducta) es (bueno/a, malo/a).

Environment (pp. 36, 42–43)

- ¿Qué debemos hacer para proteger el medio ambiente? (No) debemos/deberíamos (utilizar) (tanto vidrio). Debe haber más (contenedores para reciclar).
  Me preocupo/inquieto por (la contaminación/la polución). Sería mejor (reciclar) (más cosas). Vamos a (destrozar) (la naturaleza).

Education issues (pp. 69, 76–77)

- ¿Adónde quieres ir para seguir tus/sus estudios ? Quiero/Espero ir a (la universidad). Me gustaría hacer una carrera en (el derecho).
- ¿Qué opinas de tener reglas/normas? Creo que las reglas son (necesarias).
- ¿Hay algo que cambiarías? No estoy a favor (del uniforme).
- ¿Qué opinas de la disciplina en tu instituto? Creo que (es buena).
- ¿Cuáles son las ventajas de ir al instituto? La ventaja más grande es que (sales con buenas calificaciones).

Work, career and future plans (pp. 78, 84–85)

- ¿Qué planes tienes para el futuro? ¿En qué te gustaría trabajar? Quiero (ser comerciante). Me gustaría trabajar en el sector de (la industria). Preferiría (viajar en el extranjero). Tendré que (pedir un préstamo). Me interesa un trabajo (científico, físico, artístico).
- ¿En que trabajan tus padres? Mi madre/padre es (mecánico/a).

Social issues, choices and responsibilities (pp. 86–87)

- Los problemas sociales más importantes de hoy en día son (el paro y la guerra). Lo que más me preocupa es (la droga/el SIDA). Muy importante es (la presión del grupo paritario). Tenemos que hacer más/algo diferente para ayudar a los que (toman drogas).